Ephesians
God Calls a New People

Ephesians
God Calls a New People

David B. Howell

Smyth & Helwys Publishing, Inc.®
Macon, Georgia

ISBN 1-57312-039-1
Ephesians: God Calls a New People

David B. Howell

Copyright © 1996

Smyth & Helwys Publishing, Inc.
6316 Peake Road
Macon, Georgia 31210-3960
1-800-747-3016

Biblical quotations, unless otherwise noted, are from the
New Revised Standard Version of the Bible (NRSV).

The paper used in this publication meets the minimum
requirements of American National Standard for
Information Sciences—Permanence of Paper for Printed
Library Materials.
ANSI Z39.48–1984

Library of Congress Cataloging-in-Publication

Howell, David B.
   Ephesians: God calls a new people / David B. Howell.
   viii + 120 pp.   5.5" x 8.5"(14 x 21.5 cm.)
   Includes bibliographical references.
   ISBN 1-57312-039-1   (alk. paper)
   1. Bible. N.T. Ephesians—Criticism, interpretation, etc.
   I. Title.
   BS2695.2.H68 1996
   227'.507—dc20   96-38531
                                                        CIP

Contents

Contents

Preface

Writing never takes place in a vacuum. This was true for the New Testament letter Ephesians that we are studying; it is also true for this author and this book. We learn from a variety of sources and people. I would like to acknowledge my indebtedness to some of these in my own pilgrimage as I wrote this study guide.

I have learned much from many commentators who have written on Ephesians, but the work of Andrew T. Lincoln has been particularly stimulating as I formulated my own ideas about numerous passages in Ephesians.

Thanks are due the Adult Sunday School class at First Baptist Church of Jefferson City, Tennessee, not only for studying Ephesians while this study was being prepared, but for being a group willing to ask probing questions when studying the Bible.

My class on Paul at Carson-Newman College listened to many of the ideas in this book in the 1995 spring semester. They too provided me with questions—some of which are incorporated in the study guide. Some of my colleagues in the religion and philosophy departments read portions of the manuscript and made helpful comments.

Scott Nash has provided expert editorial assistance in making this book more readable. More significantly to me, perhaps, has been his patience over missed deadlines!

Last but not least, I must thank my family. My wife Glo has been a constant encourager and helper in our life together. Her love and support have been an indispensable undergirding for writing. The book is dedicated to our son Drew. His initial enthusiasm about Dad writing another book may have waned some when he realized it meant sharing the computer more with Dad, but throughout he has provided me with the proper mixture of encouragement and pleasant diversions needed to balance my perspective!

Introduction

One of the themes treated in the children's animated movie "The Sword in the Stone" is how a person's sense of identity can shape one's life. When the film opens, the future King Arthur of England, known as Wart, is a young boy struggling hard to work as servant and page. Unbeknownst to both the boy and his boorish masters is his true identity. Merlin the magician, however, discovers his true identity and begins to educate him. After many trials and tribulations, even mistreatment at the hands of others, the lad's identity is made plain both to himself and to the rest of the people after Wart pulls out the sword embedded in a stone. By the end of the movie he thus becomes who he is (and who he always has been): the King of England.

One of the great treatments of the theme of identity in the New Testament is found in the letter to the Ephesians. Here the readers are reminded of their identity as Christians, but this reinforcement of their sense of identity is placed in the context of prayerful praise of God's plan and work. The recipients of Ephesians are reminded that they are God's people because of God's choice and work in both creation and the church. Just as the young King Arthur in the movie must become who he is and serve as king, so also does Ephesians exhort its readers to become whom God has made them. The gift of reconciliation and the readers' place in both the church and God's purposes for the world, however, do not mean the readers have no further struggle. Ephesians also spells out the mandate for Christians to live the reconciled life both in the unity of the church and in distinctive behavior in society.

Life-Setting

Most English translations of the Bible label Ephesians with the title "The Letter of Paul to the Ephesians." Such an inscription reminds us that this "book" of the Bible is in fact not a book but a letter. As such, it was written to address Christians in a particular place and time. The letter follows the form of a Greek letter by opening with a salutation that identifies the sender and recipient of the letter (1:1-2). There is some confusion, however, about the identity of the recipients of Ephesians. Some of the oldest and best Greek manuscripts omit the words "in Ephesus." English translations that follow these manuscripts thus read "to the saints who are also faithful in Christ Jesus" (1:1).

The assumption is usually made that Paul's letters in the New Testament provide readers with a window to the relationship between the apostle and his churches. Ephesians reminds us, however, that the relationships between text, author, and recipients may be more complex.

Readership

The readers of Ephesians are clearly non-Jews, that is, Gentile Christians (see 1:1; 2:11-22; 3:1) who are members of the universal church (2:19-22; 3:6; 4:4-6). They are assumed to have known Paul, his ministry, and his suffering for the gospel (3:1-4), and he knows of their faith and love (1:15). Although the readers have experienced God's love and redemption through Christ (1:3-14), the writer's prayers for the readers suggest they are in need of encouragement. The author also prays for their growth in the knowledge, power, and love that God has made available through Jesus (1:15-23; 3:14-21).

The ethical appeals in the second half of the letter (chaps. 4–6) imply that the readers need to remember their new identity in Christ and renounce their former ways of life as non-Christians or pagans (see the use of "Gentiles" in 4:17). Christian motivation and characteristics should be active in the readers' conduct and approach to responsibilities in society (5:21–6:9). They are in a battle with hostile spiritual powers (6:10-20), but the letter emphasizes the superiority of the power of God and Christ over all the hostile powers and principalities arrayed against the church (see 1:19-23; 6:10-12).

Some commentators take the position that Ephesians is precisely what it claims to be—a letter from Paul to the church in Ephesians—but others argue that it was written perhaps by a disciple or follower of Paul. In both historical reconstructions commentators recognize the questions and problems raised by Ephesians; they end up resolving them in different ways with different explanations.

Authorship

Although the letter is ascribed to "Paul, an apostle of Christ Jesus by the will of God," questions have also arisen about Pauline authorship. Ephesians is the least personal of Paul's letters. The letter's recipients and Paul appear to have limited knowledge of one another (see 1:15; 3:2), which would be strange given the amount of time Paul spent in Ephesus ministering (see Acts 19:10; 20:18). Readers today find few references to times, places, or events in Ephesians. Moreover, the final greeting is formal and devoid of any names of fellow Christians, which one usually finds in the conclusions of Paul's letters (cf. Eph 6:21-24 with Rom 16:1-6 or 1 Cor 12:13-24).

The style and vocabulary of Ephesians are also different from other letters, with lengthy sentences that use numerous synonyms and pile word upon word. The opening prayer in Ephesians 1:3-14, for example, is one long sentence in Greek. Throughout Ephesians one finds a certain vagueness in language that seems to describe the church in abstract terms. Instead of using descriptions that help readers today situate the church in time and place, Ephesians uses language that almost describes the church as a new universe (see 1:16-23; 2:19-22; or 5:23-32). In addition, the close similarity between Colossians and Ephesians in vocabulary, structure, and thought has led some commentators to suggest that Colossians was a literary source for Ephesians that has been reworked by its author.

Most questions are raised about Pauline authorship, however, by some of the distinctive theological emphases found in Ephesians. For example, Paul usually refers to local communities of Christians when he speaks of the church or churches (Rom 16:4; 1 Cor 1:2; 4:17; 1 Thess 2:14; Phil 4:15, for example), but in Ephesians the word "church" refers to what is often called the *church universal* of Christians in all places and times (see 1:22; 3:21; 5:25, 29, 32). The problems and tensions of the relationship between Jews and Gentiles (non-Jews) in the church, which consumed so much of Paul's energy in many of his letters (see Romans and Galatians, for example), are absent in Ephesians with the union of Jew and Gentile in the church looked back upon as a past event (see 2:11-22).

Instead of talking about justification by faith in contrast to the "works of the law" (cf. Rom 3:24-28 and Gal 2:16), Ephesians generalizes the concept of salvation by grace through faith by contrasting it with "works"—that is to say, human effort (2:8-9). The verb "to justify," which is frequently used by Paul in connection with faith in other letters, is absent in Ephesians, and the noun "righteousness" appears only in the context of ethical appeals (4:24; 5:9; 6:14). The cross, a major theme in many of Paul's letters (see 1 Cor 1:18–2:5, for example), is only mentioned once in Ephesians (2:16) as the agency of reconciliation. Rather, Ephesians emphasizes Christ's resurrection and exaltation (see 1:20-23 or 4:7-16).

The author of Ephesians identifies himself as "Paul, an apostle of Christ Jesus by the will of God" (1:1). To be an apostle in the New Testament is to be one who has been sent, commissioned, and acting on behalf of the one sending (see Acts 1:20-25; Rom 1:1: 2 Cor 11:4-5). This self-designation in Ephesians 1:1 is very similar to the salutation in other letters by Paul and stresses that he speaks and acts with the authority of God (cf. 3:7-9). The author is imprisoned and suffering because of his proclamation of the gospel to the Gentiles (3:1, 13). He is a Jewish-Christian (1:12-13) who uses the Old Testament to support his claims and appeals (see 4:8; 5:14; 5:31). He is also the recipient of a revelation from God about how Jew and Gentile are united in the church (3:2-6). He asks the recipients to accept his revelation, placing himself in the company of other apostles and prophets (2:20; 3:5) but also calling himself "the very least of all the saints" (3:8).

Those who take the claims at face value that the letter was written by Paul to the church in Ephesus appeal to the traditions in the early church among the writings of the church fathers. These traditions place the letter with Paul's letters and know the letter as Ephesians. For them, this support overrides the fact that some of our best and most important Greek manuscripts omit "in Ephesus" (1:1). Some point out that in the first century in Ephesus and surrounding areas of Asia Minor (modern Turkey), the cult of Artemis and the magical practices associated with it flourished. Readers in such a life-setting would have a deep-seated fear of hostile spiritual powers, and these concerns are addressed in Ephesians. The absence of personal greetings from Paul to church members can be explained by the number of new Gentile converts who had joined the church since Paul's ministry in Ephesus. Paul did not personally know these members of the Ephesian church.

A variation of this historical reconstruction, which is found in commentaries that both support and deny Pauline authorship of the letter, argues that Ephesians was originally written as a circular letter to a number of churches—Ephesus being one of them—and a space was left in the Greek manuscript for the place of destination to be filled in. The lack of personal warmth and generalities in the letter are thus explained by the fact that Paul intended it for more than one congregation. As a circular letter it was also more appropriate for Paul to speak of the universal "church" rather than use the term to refer to a local community of believers as he normally did.

Such commentators also recognize the difference in language and theology in Ephesians when compared to other letters by Paul, but they argue that the differences are not so great as to preclude his authorship of the letter. For them, explanations are found by appealing to growth and development in Paul's thought. The different language usage and style of writing are thus not outside the range of possibility for a single author. These commentators account for some of the lofty style, lengthy sentences, and use of synonyms in Ephesians by pointing out that this is consistent with the language of prayer and praise that the letter uses.

They also argue that different theological concepts in the letter can be attributed to the situation Paul was addressing and to developments in his thought. The picture of a cosmic, exalted Christ was relevant to readers who perceived themselves as threatened by hostile spiritual powers. The image of this cosmic Christ as head of his church is consistent with the idea of the universal church and may represent a development of the metaphor of the church as the body of Christ found elsewhere in Paul's letters (see 1 Cor 12, for example).

Although Ephesians describes the church as being built on the foundation of "holy (Greek *hagiois*) apostles and prophets" (3:5; see also 2:20), this description does not necessarily represent a glance back to a bygone day and veneration of past heroes of the church. The argument is made that the term "saints" (Greek *hagioi*; see Eph 1:1) was commonly used in the early church as a designation for all Christians. In the New Testament the word is not used to describe people with special spiritual or moral qualities as we use it today, but to describe those who belong to God by virtue of God's election and activity.

Throughout the discussions in commentaries that argue for Pauline authorship of the letter, the assumption is made —whether explicitly stated or not—that the traditional ascription should be accepted unless overwhelming reasons make it impossible to do so. Markus Barth summarizes his approach to the question of authorship with the dictum "innocent until proven guilty!" A plausible life-setting for the letter must therefore be found in Paul's ministry, and Ephesians is traditionally dated between A.D. 60–62 during Paul's first imprisonment in Rome.

Other commentators, however, find implausible what these commentators arguing for Pauline authorship have found possible for one person to write and think—even for a person with as creative mind as Paul! For this second group of commentators, the differences in style and theology that we briefly outlined are too great to be the product of a single mind. For them, the most plausible life-setting for the letter is found among second-generation Christians after the death of the apostle. According to this reconstruction, Gentile Christians in the churches Paul founded in Asia Minor lost a clear sense of their identity.

Without the authority and support offered by Paul, either in person or through his letters, the Gentile Christians had become lax on moral issues. A disciple or coworker of Paul responded by writing a letter in Paul's name in order to maintain the beliefs and lifestyle of the apostles. Colossians and other letters are used for this task, but Ephesians also represents a creative adaptation and restatement of this Pauline heritage. In this new time the author of Ephesians affirms the continuity of God's work and reminds the readers of God's cosmic work and power, of their identity and membership in the universal church, of the importance of unity in the church and the role of apostles in transmitting tradition and maintaining that unity, and of the importance of maintaining an ethical identity as Christians in society.

As modern readers who think in terms of plagiarism and copyright laws, the notion of pseudonymity may strike us as deception and dishonesty. Commentators who adopt this reconstruction of the life-setting for Ephesians note, however, that the ancient world did not know about such modern concepts of intellectual property and that such practices were commonly used by both Jewish and

Christian writings. Moreover, if the letter was written after Paul's death, it is unlikely that churches he founded would have been ignorant of his demise.

More detailed discussions about the authorship and life-setting of Ephesians can be found in some of the commentaries listed in the bibliography, but I have discussed these questions to this extent in this study guide because of what Ephesians can teach us about the nature of Scripture and how it functions in the lives of Christians and the church. What does it mean to call the Bible the word of God? Where does its authority lie?

Authority

My brief discussion of attempts to reconstruct the life-setting of Ephesians, to identify its original author and readers, should underscore how sketchy and tentative our knowledge of the first century is when we are separated from it by nineteen centuries. We are reading mail originally addressed to others. How we draw an image of the letter's author and readers depends in large part on the assumptions we have when reading the Bible, assumptions about the nature of the Bible and how great a diversity in thought and style is possible within the mind of a single individual. Is it necessary, however, for the named author of a biblical book or letter to be the actual author for the Bible still to be God's word as some people claim? Is Ephesians, for example, less authoritative if Paul did not write it?

Some commentators argue that the question of authorship has no impact upon the inspiration or authority of Ephesians. To argue otherwise places more emphasis on *who* wrote a text than *what* it says. Writing is a human activity, and inspiration should not mean the processes and conventions utilized to produce a text were neglected or not respected. Part of the miracle and scandal of revelation is the particularity of God's revelation of God through human agency. Preeminent is the incarnation, whereby God became human in His son Jesus, but God also speaks in the Bible produced by human hands that represent responses to God's revelation and work.

Authority is always relational and communal, and closely connected to the idea of biblical authority is the concept of canon. A *canon* is a normative collection of writings that serve as an authoritative source for a religious community's faith and practice. For the Christian church, our canon includes both the Old Testament and the New Testament; the latter are writings produced by Christians in response to God's work in Christ. Although the church produced these documents, these writings also stand over and above the community. Here they help shape our identity both as individual Christians and as a community. Here they mediate God's presence. Here they provide us with the language of faith to help convey our experience of God's presence.

Ephesians is a part of this collection that has shaped the church's identity and guided it through the centuries irrespective of its authorship. While the letter we know as Ephesians was written in a specific context in the first century, the message and theology of Ephesians transcend a particular place and time whether written by Paul or one of his followers. Ephesians is powerful because both then and now its readers need to be reminded of God's work and plan for creation and the church, of their identity and distinct ethical qualities as Christians in church and society. Ephesians is God's word because God continues to speak through this letter.

Ephesians can thus be authoritative for Christians today, even if Paul did not write the letter, because of its capacity to mediate God's presence and because of its usefulness to the church in helping shape Christian identity. When we speak of biblical authority in this manner, we should not think of the Bible acting independently in a vacuum. To recognize its authority is to read it in the context of a community of faith under the guidance of the Holy Spirit. The Holy Spirt that is believed to be active when the biblical documents were written must be affirmed as continuing to work today as Christians read Ephesians. There is therefore the convergence of the witnesses of the Bible, of church tradition, and of the Holy Spirit working in the lives of Christians.

If modern readers follow the historical reconstruction that postulates a follower of Paul as the actual author of Ephesians, then he wrote in Paul's name to apply the apostle's thought to a new situation. Ephesians thus might be conceived of as a "recontextualization," as Darrell Joddock terms it, of Paul's ideas and advice. To illustrate this concept, Joddock uses the analogy of a child listening to her mother's advice who must then decide when faced with a new situation what action would be appropriate in order to be true to that advice. Christians are confronted with the act of recontextualization every Sunday when we attend church and listen to the minister's sermon that takes the Bible and addresses our situation in the twentieth century. Without the need for such a recontextualization there would be no need for a sermon. And when we study Ephesians and God speaks to us today through a letter written in the first century, recontextualization happens whether the letter was penned by Paul or one of his associates.

Despite the tentativeness of our knowledge of the first-century church and because of the hazardous nature of specifying author and readers of this letter, I will follow tradition and refer to the author of Ephesians throughout the study guide as Paul and the letter's recipients as the Ephesians. By these terms, however, I mean the literary Paul and the literary Ephesians. You the reader can decide for yourself the precise relationship between these encoded figures and the real flesh-and-blood author and readers!

Structure and Purpose

As we turn to read Ephesians, we should be sensitive to how Paul structures the letter and addresses his readers. Although the opening salutation of Ephesians is similar to the greeting used in other letters by the apostle (and basically conforms to the form of an ancient Greek letter), the body of the letter is different. Usually in Paul's letters (following the conventions of Greek letters), the opening is followed by a prayer of thanksgiving, the body of the letter, a section of moral exhortation, and a conclusion. In Ephesians, however, chapter 1 has two prayers (vv. 3-14 and 15-23), and chapter 3 concludes with a prayer of intercession (vv. 14-21). In addition, the section of moral exhortation has been expanded, and Paul's ethical advice is found in chapters 4–6.

As a result, commentators are unsure about where to locate the body of the letter. There is broad agreement, however, that Ephesians can be divided into two fundamental parts: the first half of the letter is a prayer section (chaps. 1–3), and the second half is ethical advice (chaps. 4–6). These two sections should not be construed as rigid categories that are self-contained, discrete units. Ethical concerns are present in the prayer section, and prayer and theology undergird the ethical advice. The structure of Ephesians with its order reminds us, however, of a basic truth of the Christian life.

In the first half of the letter we find the interpretation of faith leaping to worship in grateful praise to God, which then becomes the foundation for ethical reflection in the second half. Without such an order, ethical maxims risk the danger of becoming something externally imposed that can lead to a legalism. The alternative vision offered in Ephesians is to see ethical behavior springing forth internally through the transformation of a person in Christ.

When we read Ephesians, we need to pay attention not only to the structure of the letter, but also to how Paul uses language. When and how does he pray, theologize, persuade, or offer ethical advice in Ephesians? The philosopher Ludwig Wittgenstein compared words to tools. Just as we can use tools for diverse functions, we use sentences or paragraphs for different purposes; we can bless or curse, ask or command, narrate a story or write explanatory prose.

We notice in reading Ephesians that Paul has a number of different "tools" or types of argumentation in his "toolbox" of words to remind and reinforce his readers' identity as Christians. Andrew Lincoln has identified three different types of rhetorical language in the letter: the language of thanksgiving and prayer (worship), the language of recalling the past (*anamnesis*), and the language of ethical exhortation (*parenesis*).

The language of worship and the language of anamnesis are used predominately in the first half of the letter. In this extended prayer section Paul constructs a world through prayer and praise that enthrones God. In this world Christ has defeated the powers of the present evil age and equipped the church to live and work. The language of recall is also used, especially in chapter 2, as Paul reminds the readers of their own experiences of God's work of reconciliation through Jesus. Using language in these ways enables Paul to connect to his readers—prayer, for example, is an effective way to express concern—and affirm shared beliefs and values. It also allows him to build a platform from which he can address his ethical exhortations in the second half of the letter.

Many commentators have referred to the first half of Ephesians as the doctrinal section while the second half is the practical section. The careful reader of Ephesians, however, will take note of how Paul uses language of worship and recall in the first half of the letter to develop his theology. A doctrine of election verbalized by a Christian in an act of praise and thanksgiving (1:3-14), for example, is quite different from a doctrine of predestination developed with calculated logic in theological prose as we shall see later in this study guide.

Readers need to be careful about how phrases and concepts are lifted out of the relationship between a grateful speaker and a gracious God and objectified to serve some theological dogma. On the other hand, much theology is transmitted through worship because worship addresses not just the intellect but also the emotions. Consider, for example, how the hymns we sing in church today shape what many people believe. Worship as a way of theological discourse is effective precisely because people are moved to believe and act in certain ways. Ephesians thus not only reminds us of a fruitful way to construct theology today; it also warns us with its language of worship to be careful how we appropriate the Bible in theological formulations.

Paul's choice of these three different strategies and modes of theologizing in Ephesians (that is, the language of worship, recall, and moral exhortation) underscore what I perceive to be central ideas in the letter: the readers' identity and calling as Christians. Paul writes Ephesians as a pastor who wants to persuade the readers. Through the language of worship and recall, the Ephesians' identity is rooted in God's purposes (see 1:3-14). As Christians they share in Christ's risen life that frees them from enslavement to the powers of this world (see 2:6) and yet also leads them into conflict with these powers. The second half of Ephesians with its moral advice, therefore, calls upon the Ephesians to live out their identity in ethical purity (notice 4:1, 17; 5:2, 8, 15 and the repeated use of the verb "to walk"). Because this identity is set within the wider context of God's redeeming work in Christ, however, it is not an individualist identity but one that is developed in community within the church.

Reading Ephesians Today

Since we are not the original recipients of Ephesians, I suggest that we use the concept of recontextualization discussed earlier as a helpful model for understanding how we read the letter today. The questions and experiences we bring to the letter in the twentieth century are not those of first-century readers of Ephesians. We need to recognize this historical distance and try to understand Ephesians in its first-century context. What was its message and impact then? Interpretation does not stop here, however, without the second step of considering how Ephesians' message and vision of Christian identity can be appropriated in the twentieth century.

This study guide should help readers with the first step as we explore the world that Ephesians portrays. I will also make some suggestions about how these insights from Ephesians' world can impact the world of the contemporary reader. Because readers will bring different experiences and questions to the reading process, however, my comments about the second step will be more suggestive. Perhaps they will prime the pump of your imagination (as you read Ephesians and this study guide) so that you may recontextualize Ephesians for God to speak to your specific contemporary situation.

Questions for Reflection

1. In what ways is Ephesians different from other letters written by Paul?

2. If Ephesians was not written by Paul, who wrote it, and why was it written? Why do other commentators think that Paul was the author of the letter?

3. What does it mean to consider the Bible authoritative? Where does its authority lie, and how does it function in the church and lives of Christians today?

4. What different ways does Paul use language in Ephesians to persuade his readers? Does the church continue to use language in these ways today? If so, how? Can you think of other functions of language in church?

For Further Reading

Arnold, C. E. *Ephesians: Power and Magic*. SNTSMS 63. Cambridge: Cambridge University Press, 1989.

Barth, Markus. *Ephesians*. 2 vols. Anchor Bible 34. New York: Doubleday, 1974.

Bruce, F. F. *The Epistles to the Colossians, to Philemon, and to the Ephesians*. New International Commentary of the New Testament. Grand Rapids MI: Eerdmans, 1984.

Brueggemann, Walter. *Israel's Praise: Doxology against Idolatry and Ideology*. Philadelphia: Fortress, 1988.

Joddock, Darrell. *The Church's Bible: Its Contemporary Authority*. Philadelphia: Fortress, 1989.

Johnson, Luke T. *The Writings of the New Testament: An Interpretation*. Philadelphia: Fortress, 1986.

Lincoln, Andrew T. *Ephesians*. Word Biblical Commentary 42. Waco TX: Word, 1990.

Lincoln, A. T. and A. J. M. Wedderburn. *The Theology of the Later Pauline Letters*. Cambridge: Cambridge University Press, 1993.

Martin, Ralph P. *Ephesians, Colossians, and Philemon*. Interpretation Commentaries. Louisville KY: John Knox, 1992.

Martin, Ralph P. "Ephesians." *Broadman Bible Commentary*. Vol. 11. Nashville TN: Broadman, 1971.

Meade, David G. *Pseudonymity and Canon: An Investigation into the Relationship of Authorship and Authority in Jewish and Earliest Christian Tradition*. WUNT 39. Tübingen: Mohr, 1986.

Mitton, C. L. *Ephesians*. New Century Bible. Grand Rapids MI: Eerdmans, 1973.

Schnackenburg, R. *The Epistle to the Ephesians*. Edinburgh: T & T Clark, 1991.

Smith, T. C. *How We Got Our Bible*. Macon GA: Smyth & Helwys, 1994.

Tolbert, Malcolm. *Ephesians: God's New People*. Nashville TN: Convention Press, 1979.

Wittgenstein, Ludwig. *Philosphical Investigation*. I, #11. Oxford: Blackwell, 1958.

Chapter 1

Praise and Intercession
Identity and Calling

Ephesians 1:3-23

Go to almost any church, and the worship service will include songs and prayers of praise and thanksgiving. The songs may be traditional hymns or contemporary choruses, but in both cases the worship is a joyous and grateful expression in response to God's power and mercy. Walter Brueggemann argues in his book on the Psalms that Israel's prayers and hymns of praise are offered not only in response to God's action in the world. They do more than merely celebrate God's presence and deliverance. According to Brueggemann, they also create a world where God reigns so that praise is an attack on idolatry and the powers of other gods.

In Ephesians we find a similar use of praise. Paul offers the readers a vision of reality and Christian existence in which God has enthroned Christ, defeated the powers opposing God, and made available to Christians the resources to stand firm and grow. Just as preachers of positive thinking today ask people to imagine themselves successfully accomplishing some task, so Paul hopes that the Ephesians get caught up in the world created through praise so that they can live out the new life God has made possible. The prayers in the opening chapter of Ephesians introduce this alternative world developed in the letter.

Praise for God's Purposes for Salvation in Christ
(1:3-14)

Paul usually follows the conventions of Greek letter-writing by offering a prayer of thanksgiving for the recipients of the letter after the opening salutation (1:1-2). Ephesians is different, however, for here we find two prayers in chapter 1. The second prayer (1:15-23) parallels the normal prayer of thanksgiving with its intercessory elements, but it is preceded in Ephesians by a prayer of blessing to God (1:3-14). These opening prayers help set the tone for the letter with its many hymnic and liturgical elements. They also introduce important themes and ideas that will be dealt with later in the letter. In Ephesians, theology and ethical exhortations are set in the context of worship and praise.

The pattern for the opening prayer of Ephesians is found in the Jewish prayer of blessing (Hebrew *berakah*) used in synagogues. These prayers had three parts—an opening statement of praise, reasons for the praise, and a conclusion of renewed praise—that are paralleled in Ephesians. The *berakah* functioned primarily as an act of remembrance. The prayer was not offered, however, simply out of curious interest for past events. Rather, its purpose was to make the past active and relevant for the present of those offering the praise.

In synagogue worship Jews praised the God who had acted so graciously in Israel's past with the expectation that God could also be trusted to be active and loving in the present and future. In Ephesians the language of election, predestination, and God's plan in the blessing speak to the readers' identity as Christians and thus lay the foundation for the exhortation later in the letter "to lead a life worthy of the calling to which you have been called" (4:1).

Although most English translations divide the opening prayer of praise into numerous sentences for the sake of clarity, it is one long sentence in Greek. The prayer is not without structure, however. It is punctuated with periodic responses of praise (vv. 6, 12, 14), and commentators see a logical development in the reasons offered for blessing God. After the opening statement of praise, some see a chronological development in the pattern of praise. Paul moves through time, beginning with God's purposes in eternity before the foundation of the world (v. 4), through God's redeeming work of Jesus (v. 7), to the personal experiences of forgiveness and receiving of the spirit by the readers of Ephesians (v. 13).

Others offer an alternative trinitarian outline for the blessing, noting that the praise moves from the electing purposes of God the father to the work of Christ the son and the activity of the Holy Spirit. The perspective on the Trinity operative here is not the theological dogma of later church councils, however, with their reflection on God's essence or being. Rather, the Trinitarian perspective is essentially functional in nature as it focuses on God's different actions. The two alternative patterns to the prayer of blessing should thus not be viewed as mutually exclusive, for they supplement and support one another. God's redeeming work in the earthly ministry, death, and resurrection lies in the past of the recipients of Ephesians, but God's redemptive presence in their lives is now realized through the work of the Spirit.

If the blessing of 1:3-14 introduces key words and ideas used throughout the letter, verse 3 as the opening declaration of praise serves as a programmatic statement with themes developed in the blessing. The blessing is *theocentric* (God-centered), directed to God who is the source of salvation. Paul has taken this particular Jewish form of praise, however, and given it a Christian character by also focusing on Christ as God's agent who brings about this salvation. When God is addressed as the "Father of our Lord Jesus Christ" (1:3), father is used as a metaphor that is relational in nature. The term brings to mind images of familial love and respect. Jesus also referred to God as father (see Matt 6:1, 4, 6, 8-9, 14-15, for example, or Luke 24:34, 36). When the metaphor is connected to Jesus as it is here in Ephesians, however, it underscores the special relationship between Jesus and God. This relationship and Jesus' work make it possible for Christians to be adopted as God's children and address God as "father."

The content of the blessing is summed up in the three prepositional phrases in 1:3 that use the Greek preposition *en* (in). The phrase "in Christ" or one of its variations ("in him," for example) help give the blessing its specifically Christian character as they are used eleven times in the opening prayer. The phrase "in Christ" is frequently found in Paul's letters, and commentators debate the precise sense of the phrase. Here it is most likely used in an instrumental sense (that is, *by means of Christ*), although a local sense is also possible (that is, Christians are incorporated *into the body of* Christ and thus share his blessings). In the prayer of praise it helps underscore that the blessings are possible because of the gift of grace.

The second prepositional phrase in the string characterizes the blessing as "spiritual." This description is appropriate not because the blessings are only concerned with the inner person in contrast to the outer, physical person. Rather, they are "spiritual" because they are connected with the work of the Holy Spirit (see the conclusion of the blessing at 1:13-14, which specifically addresses the work of the Spirit).

The final prepositional phrase in the series of prepositions in the opening declaration of praise places the spiritual blessings "in the heavenly places." The word, which in Greek literally means "the heavenlies," appears five times in Ephesians (see also 1:20; 2:6; 3:10; and 6:12). The spiritual blessings are placed here because they derive from Christ, the church's head who has been raised from the dead and reigns from heaven (see 1:20). Malcolm Tolbert's assertion in an earlier study guide of Ephesians that the prepositional phrase refers to relationship rather than geography is one way of making sense of this perspective for twentieth-century readers who may be operating with a view of the universe different from a first-century cosmology. Because Christians are incorporated into Christ and participate in his resurrection, Paul breaks forth in such a panoply of praise.

One final note of interest in the opening declaration of blessing in 1:3 is Paul's use of first person plural pronouns ("our" and "us"). Except for the alternation with the second person pronoun "you" in 1:13, Paul uses first person pronouns throughout this *berakah*. The pronoun in the prayer is inclusive and not exclusive so that Paul refers to all Christians as the recipients of God's grace and blessings. The plural pronoun also reminds us, however, that while God's blessings are personal, they are not private and individualistic. The perspective of the church and communal dimension of Christian existence, which is important throughout Ephesians, is thus also introduced in the opening doxology.

God is praised by Paul because God is the giver of blessings. Some of these blessings—election, adoption, redemption, forgiveness, salvation, the work of the Holy Spirit—are enumerated in the prayer (1:4-14). As Paul lists these reasons for blessing God, the reader is struck by the vast expanse of Paul's perspective. He incorporates all possible dimensions of time in his praise, from the pretemporal (v. 4) to the future consummation (v. 14). Moreover, God's purposes embrace the entire universe (1:9-10).

The emphasis in the prayer is on God's plan, and Paul uses a number of different words in the blessing to express volition: verbs such as "chose" (v. 4), "destined" (vv. 5, 11), "purposed" or "set forth" (v. 9), "appointed" (v. 11); and nouns such as "will" (v. 5, 9, 11), "purpose" or "good pleasure" (vv. 5, 9), "plan" (v. 10), and "counsel" (v. 11). Although the language used by Paul in this blessing has been at the center of controversies throughout the history of theology, the blessing itself does not reflect the subsequent debates about divine sovereignty and free will, about the positive and negative aspects of God's election (that is to say, whether God chooses some for salvation and dooms others to damnation).

What the blessing does affirm first and foremost is that God is the source and origin of the spiritual blessings. The emphasis on God's purpose stresses that salvation was not by chance, dependent upon some spur-of-the-moment decision by God in reaction to events or human actions. Rather, these blessings were planned by God "before the foundation of the world" (1:4) and focused in Christ (1:4-5, 9-10).

By stressing the pretemporal nature of what we call election, the blessing secondly underscores the element of grace at work. In the blessing, Paul's language of choice and volition is a way of affirming that the initiative for becoming a Christian always lies with God. God's choice is not a reward for human merit, but is "rooted in the depth of God's nature." Although the Greek is ambiguous about whether the prepositional phrase "in love" at the end of 1:4 goes with what precedes it or what follows it, many translations render it with the verb in 1:5 and so read "he destined us in love" (RSV). This understanding of the passage makes the blessing closely parallel the assertion in John 3:16, the verse that most people first learned in Sunday School as small children, that "God so loved the world that he gave he only begotten Son that whoever believes in him shall not perish but have eternal life."

Third, the blessing's emphasis on God's initiative in salvation does not absolve the Christian from responsible, moral behavior. This idea is expressed in a number of different ways in the passage. God's electing purposes have the goal that Christians be "holy and blameless before him" (1:4). Andrew Lincoln argues in his commentary that the prepositional phrase "in love" goes with this verse so that the terms holy, blameless, and love (understood now as a human act) compliment each other. These nouns not only describe the character of Christians, who are to be both separated from sin (just as sacrifices in the Old Testament were to be blameless, without defect or blemish) and active in love, they also provide a thumbnail summary of the ethical exhortations that are developed in the second half of the letter in chapters 4–6.

God's election also has the goal of making Christians "sons" (1:5). The Greek word used means "adopted as sons." To be a son was to have sovereignty and freedom in contrast to servants and slaves. To be an adopted child (Paul wrote before the days of gender-inclusive language!), however, does not simply mean that one receives privileges

with no responsibility. The same word is used by Paul in
Romans 9:4 of Israel, and the Old Testament makes clear
that Israel was chosen by God not merely for its benefit but
so that God might use Israel for God's service (see Exod
19:4-6, for example).

Adoption as children is one of the spiritual blessings
God has freely given Christians through Jesus (1:6, 8).
Other benefits that are a present experience for believers
are listed in 1:7-10. "Redemption" (1:7) is a word rooted in
the Old Testament in Israel's experience of deliverance and
liberation by God from Egypt in the Exodus. The phrase
"forgiveness from our trespasses" is parallel to redemption
and specifies a primary way in which Christians experience
God's deliverance. Although Paul more typically speaks of
sin in the singular as an enslaving power opposed to God,
he also uses it in the plural to refer to acts of disobedience
and transgression (see Rom 4:25 or 2 Cor 5:19, for example). Believers have also been given "all wisdom and
insight" to understand and live the new life God has graciously lavished on them. We should not think of this
knowledge as mere intellectual or cognitive understanding,
for it also entails an experiential dimension based upon the
relationship between a person and God and should result
in moral behavior.

Part of what Christians are to know is described in 1:9
as "the mystery of his will." Andrew Lincoln argues in his
commentary that 1:9-10 plays a crucial part in the opening
doxology because these verses underscore the comprehen-
sive nature of God's action in Christ. The term "mystery"
would have sounded familiar to the ears of the letter's
recipients since it was used in both Jewish and pagan religions to refer to a previously hidden secret that God has
chosen to reveal. The term, in fact, gave the name to a

group of religions in the ancient world known as the "mystery religions." They were characterized by a group of secrets known only by those initiated into the religion.

In contrast to these religions, which usually referred to the "mysteries" in the plural, Paul uses the singular form. The "secret" involves what God is doing through Christ. It is a mystery that not only has been revealed to Christians, but one whose significance affects the entire world, not just its own religious community. It is also a secret that can be openly proclaimed (6:19).

In Christ, God is working to restore harmony to the cosmos, and those who are in Christ are a part of this wider program. The blessing thus serves as a word of assurance, counteracting insecurities raised by a fragmented and hostile world by affirming that nothing in earth is outside of God's redemptive purposes. The harmony and unity between Jew and Gentile in the church, which Paul develops later in Ephesians (2:11-22 and 3:9-10, for example), is present evidence of God's plan.

The recipients of Ephesians are explicitly brought into the blessing in 1:13 by Paul's use of the second person pronoun "you." Commentators have explained the switch from "we" (1:12) to "you" in a number of ways. For some, the switch represents a contrast between Jews and the Gentile readers of the letter. For others, the contrast is between first-generation and second-generation Christians. The Jew / Gentile contrast is not introduced until chapter 2, and Paul reverts back to first person pronouns in 1:14. Both believers in general and the recipients of the letter specifically receive the same blessing with the acceptance of the gospel and the gift of the Holy Spirit.

Although the emphasis in Ephesians is on the present reality of God's blessing in Christian existence, Paul's comments about the Holy Spirit in 1:13-14 reveal the tension between the "already and not yet" of Christian existence that is characteristic of Paul's letters. To be "sealed" with the Spirit is to be marked as God's special possession just as cattle might be branded as a sign of ownership. When does this sealing take place? Some have argued that water baptism was the moment, but it is preferable to see the reference to the reception of the Spirit, which all Christians receive, without tying it to a specific occasion (although in the early church this event was closely associated with baptism).

Paul also decribes the Spirit as a "guarantee" (1:14). This was a commercial word that referred to a down payment or earnest money for a purchase. The present experience of the Spirit is not the complete inheritance. More is yet to come. Christians thus exist between two dimensions —heaven and earth (cf. Phil 3:20-21)—and two ages—the present age and the age to come. In Ephesians those who are seated with Christ in the heavenly realms (2:10; cf. 1:3) must also do battle with hostile spiritual powers (6:11-20), even though they share in Christ's victory.

The opening blessing of God, however, constructs a world through praise that is foundational for the rest of the letter. In this world the readers' identity is rooted in God's purposes, which have been realized through Christ's work. The blessing functions to give the readers assurance that God's redemptive purposes and actions are sufficient and offer more than any other power or gods can. The frequent declarations to praise God in the doxology suggest, however, that praising God is also a fundamental characteristic of Christian existence (1:6, 12, 14). The readers are reminded of the blessings of God so that they may respond in gratitude and praise.

When we read this opening prayer in Ephesians today, it should remind us not to neglect praise and worship as ways of shaping Christian identity and doing theology. When we respond in grateful thanksgiving for what God has done, we are not only brought into the presence of a living and transforming God, we also invite others to join us in this presence. In this presence, the power of competing gods and hostile interests lose its efficacy so that the world we have praised into existence becomes a reality, transforming the present world through a message of reconciliation and the work of justice. Because the praise is centered on God, we are reminded that ultimately God is behind all our efforts, undergirding our work.

We need to be reminded as well that whatever doctrine of election is to be found in this passage, it is expressed through the language of worship and set in the context of praise. This is a different way of doing theology from writing in abstract prose. Here in Ephesians, election serves to assure rather than puzzle.

Prayer for the Church
(1:15-23)

Thanksgiving and praise merge into intercession as Paul moves to the second prayer in the opening chapter of Ephesians. Like the opening prayer of blessing, this prayer is also one long sentence in Greek, and it has numerous overlaps with the earlier blessing. It can be divided into three parts: a prayer of thanksgiving (1:15-16a), intercessions for the recipients (1:16b-19), and a confessional praise for Christ's work and exaltation (1:20-23). It functions in the letter to take up elements of the earlier blessing and to pray that the recipients of Ephesians might grow in their knowledge and experience of the blessings enumerated.

We thus find in the opening chapter the dual movement characteristic of Christian identity and prayer; one gives grateful thanks and praise for the gifts of God's grace already received but also asks for more gifts and blessing. Christianity should be a journey in which one is never satisfied with the status quo. The coming kingdom of God, which for Christians is also a present reality, calls them into the future of an ever new and growing relationship with God.

This new prayer begins with a glance back at the preceding blessing ("for this reason") and is a consequence of all that God has done. The reasons given for Paul's thanksgiving are the recipients' "faith in the Lord Jesus and your love toward all the saints." The manner with which these qualities have come to Paul's attention (that is, by hearing) implies a lack of firsthand knowledge by the apostle. Numerous commentators have seized on this impression as evidence that either Paul was not the author of the letter (if it was directed to the church at Ephesus) or that the letter was originally a circular letter written to a number of churches.

The two qualities mentioned are general Christian characteristics, but together they imply two different dimensions or relationships of Christian faith. There is a vertical dimension whereby the Christian stands in relationship with God. This relationship is expressed here in the expression "faith in the Lord Jesus." It also connects to language in the blessing where the recipients "believed in him" (1:13). In the New Testament the term *faith* does not primarily refer to intellectual assent to certain doctrines.

Rather, the structure of faith involves both a *trust* in God and *obedience.*

Obedience to God is not merely directed vertically to God. Christians obey and love God also in their relationships to other people. In both Jesus' and Paul's teaching this ethic can be summarized by the word love. The horizontal dimension of Christian life in relation to others is thus expressed in 1:15 in the expression of "love for all the saints." Although some Greek manuscripts omit the word "love," the sentence makes no sense without it and most translations following the reading that includes it. We might do well "to verb" the noun love because in the New Testament love is an active, "practical concern for the welfare of another" and not simply a tenderhearted emotion. The other persons in this verse are identified as "saints," which is the same word used in the letter's salutation (1:1). It refers to all of God's people.

The prayer of thanksgiving itself commences with an introduction that whenever Paul prays, he remembers the readers in intercessory prayer (1:16). The language is similar to that used in other letters of Paul (see Phil 1:3; 1 Thess 1:2-3, 9), which combine to paint a portrait of an apostle who did not remain detached and aloof from churches he ministered in. Paul continued to remain interested and active in the lives of Christians even after he departed from a city through means of letters, visits from coworkers, and prayer.

The essence of the prayer is that the readers might come to a deeper understanding of what God has accomplished for them. In 1:8 God is blessed for providing believers with "wisdom and insight." This language is taken up in the intercessory prayer so that the readers may grow in "wisdom" and "revelation of knowledge" (1:17). It is interesting to note that although later in the letter Paul (3:3) and holy apostles and prophets (3:5) are the recipients of revelation, God's revelation is not limited to them. Here God's revelation is also directed to all Christians.

Paul continues to pray for illumination and understanding in verse 18 because in biblical anthropology (view of humans), the heart was the center of the will and intellect. This knowledge has a threefold content in which readers should be aware not only of the future (that is, "the hope of their calling" and "the riches of the glorious inheritance"), but also of the present reality of God's power. The piling up of synonyms for God's power in 1:19 suggests that it is the ultimacy and efficacy of this great power that Paul wants the Ephesians to appreciate. Their hope and calling are secure because God's purposes are being actualized.

Intercession shifts over to praise in 1:20-23. The supreme demonstration of the power that is available to believers is found in Christ's resurrection from the dead. The emphasis in the praise is not on Christ's resurrection, however, but on his exaltation where he sits enthroned in heaven at God's right hand. The language, drawn from Psalms 110:1, is frequently used in the New Testament of Christ (see Rom 8:34; 1 Cor 15:25, for example).

To sit at the right hand was to sit at a place of power and to exercise sovereignty. Christ's sovereignty is made clear here by the enumeration of the various vanquished cosmic powers Christ has defeated. The defeated powers are both of this age and the age to come (1:21), a common Jewish way of speaking of the present and the future. The language emphasizes the universality and finality of Christ's victory. Verse 22a sums up the supremacy of Christ's exalted status with a quote from Psalms 8:6, "He has put all things under his feet." What is distinctive about Paul's use of this quotation in Ephesians is that the subjection is viewed as a completed event (contrast this perspective with 1 Cor 15:24-28, which also combines Pss 110 and 8 but from the perspective of the end of time). Paul's perspective here in Ephesians is no doubt colored by the type of language used at this point in the letter.

For Christians in Asia Minor where magic flourished and belief in hostile spiritual powers was common, Paul's praise of Christ's exaltation was intended to assure. That God's power that raised and exalted Christ is available and at work in God's people is made explicit in 1:22b with the mention of the church. This verse is the first mention in the letter of *ekklesia*, a key word in Ephesians. In the Greek translation of the Old Testament, this word is the primary word used to translate the Hebrew *qahal* and refers to the *assembly* of the people of Israel in covenant with God.

In the New Testament, the term *ekklesia* is most frequently used to refer to a local group of believers. In Ephesians, however, all nine occurences of the word refer to the universal church (that is, the totality of believers). Church and Christ are thus both placed in cosmic perspective, and Paul makes the startling claim that Christ's supremacy over the cosmos was given for the benefit of believers. This is the reason that Christians do not have to be in bondage to other gods and powers.

In describing Christ as head, Paul also describes the church as his body. This image highlights the interdependence of the community with each other (see 1 Cor 12) and with Christ. Since Ephesians has the totality of believers in mind, however, the main thrust of the image is the living and dynamic relationship between Christ and his people, which is life-sustaining. The church is his body, however, and as head he is Lord over it.

The last two clauses of 1:23, "the fullness of him who fills all in all," are fraught with interpretive difficulties. Does the word "fullness" describe Christ's body (that is, the church) or Christ? Who does the filling? Does Christ fill the church? Does the church fill Christ? Or is Christ filled by God? Commentators who opt for the first choice see the church as the fullness of Christ, which he fills by his dynamic headship and with special gifts (cf. Eph 4:7-11). Commentators who opt for the second choice of the church filling Christ usually see this filling happening when the church goes on its mission. As Christ's body, the church is his hands and feet and voice that do his work.

Whichever intepretation is followed, and the first option where Christ fills the church is the most common one, the opening prayers of Ephesians end on high note for the church that both affirm the church's significance and its dependency on Christ. God's purposes in Christ for the world are now being realized in the church.

The prayers of Ephesians 1 use language that is not limited to a particular location. The perspective is grand and sweeping. Perhaps it is this grandeur of the vision that has made the message and theology of Ephesians so powerful throughout the church's history. Through praise Paul has portrayed what God has done in Christ. Through prayer he asks the readers to grow in their awareness and knowledge of these blessings and become who God has called them to be. Christian identity is rooted in God's initiative and activity. Paul's prayer is that we may appropriate that calling.

Questions for Reflection

1. What is the purpose of the blessing in 1:3-14? How does a doctrine of election function in such a prayer?

2. What words does the blessing use to describe the benefits of salvation? In what sense are these a present reality, and in what sense do they lie in the future?

3. What is the mystery of God's plan that has now been made known (1:9-10)?

4. What does Paul pray for in the intercessory prayer for the Ephesians (1:15-23)?

5. What "powers" today keep you from appropriating the blessings of God's work in Christ?

Chapter 2

Once and Now

Ephesians 2:1-22

The once-now contrast must include all we are: the conversion of our ancestors in the distant past, the intervening elements of Christian history, both good and bad, which have nonetheless preserved the gospel and the church through the ages, our baptism and Christian upbringing, our nurture and our own experiences.

—Nils A. Dahl

How common it is to switch on the television to a Christian program or go to a revival meeting at church and hear people telling their stories of how Christ changed their lives. The more dramatic the change is from one's previous life of crime or addiction to drugs or alcohol to becoming a law-abiding, caring, and devout person, the more vivid and arresting the testimony will be. These stories of contrast give voice to the efficacy of the life-changing power of what God has done in Christ. They also draw upon the same schema of once/now, past/present that Paul uses in the opening verses of Ephesians 2. The language of prayer used in the blessing and thanksgiving of chapter 1 is replaced with a different type of language of worship, the language of recall, in chapter 2. The two chapters are connected, however. Paul's eulogy and prayer of thanksgiving for what God has accomplished in Christ moves him to remind his readers of their own past. He reminds them of the contrast between their former lives and their present experience of salvation (2:1-10), before recounting the past in more general terms of the previous alienation of Jew and Gentile that has been overcome in the church by the reconciling work of Christ (2:11-22).

Transformed Lives: From Death to Life
(2:1-10)

Paul asks his readers to remember their past from the perspective of their present experiences of the blessings of salvation. In 2:1-3 he describes their condition before their experience of Christ's transforming power. Verses 4-10 then spell out the change Christ has made in their lives. These verses contain some of the most theologically powerful statements in Ephesians of God's redemptive work in Jesus.

We find the same alternation between the second person and first person pronouns in this chapter that was used in the first chapter of Ephesians. Does the "you" in 2:1-2, for example, function to draw attention to the specific experience of the readers, which is then widened to include the experiences of all Christians in 2:3 with the use of "we"? Or is Paul making a distinction between the experience of Jews and Gentiles with the different pronouns in chapter 2?

One can perhaps make a better case for the latter interpretation in this chapter than for this reading in Ephesians 1 because the readers—"you"—are specifically identified in 2:11-22 as Gentiles. If this understanding is followed, Paul argues in a way similar to Romans 1-3. There too the sinful condition of Gentiles is discussed (1:18-32) before Paul turns to argue that Jews are also sinners. Romans 3 contains the joint indictment of Gentile and Jew as sinner (see v. 9), just as Ephesians 2:3 argues that Gentile and Jew suffer the same predicament. The inclusive nature of the first person plural pronoun throughout 2:1-11 (see vv. 4, 5, 7, 10), however, suggests that we need to be cautious about making too sharp a distinction between the experiences of Jew and Gentile as represented by different pronouns.

Paul uses the metaphors of death and life in this opening section of chapter 2 to contrast the conditions of his readers before and after their experience of salvation. Since life is found in God alone, death characterizes those who are alienated from God. Paul portrays this spiritual death or alienation in terms of being subject to hostile spiritual powers (see 2:2 and the depiction of "the prince of the power of the air"). Elsewhere in Ephesians this personal center of evil is identified as the devil (see 4:27; 6:11), which is an atypical designation for Paul. Far more common in his letters is the name Satan.

The tyranny of sin that humanity lives under is not just external, however. It is also internal as Paul describes in a number of different ways how the readers once were in active rebellion against God and thus responsible for their actions. They chose not to obey ("sons of disobedience" in 2:2 is a description of those whose life is characterized by disobedience). Instead, they lived (the meaning of "walk" in 2:2 is a mode of conduct) by following the passions and desires of the "flesh" (2:3).

Paul uses two different words for sin in 2:1. *Hamartia* means to miss the mark or target one was aiming at, whereas *paraptoma* usually means concrete acts of transgression or trespass. Here the two words mean the same for all practical purposes and are an example of the author's love of synonyms in this letter. It is more usual, however, to find in Paul's letter sin used in the singular as an almost abstract power that enslaves humanity; that is to say, it is a sphere of existence characterized by enmity to God. C. K. Barrett thus writes that "sin is primarily a relational rather than an ethical word . . . defined not in relation to an ethical system but in relation to God."[1] The opposite of sin thus understood is not virtue, but faith (see Rom 14:23). This

understanding is not to say, however, that to be in rebellion to God has no ethical consequences because to disobey
God is to miss the good God intends for creation (although
conversely, Christians have not cornered the market on
virtuous behavior).

Another word employed by Paul to describe the human
condition in the past of pre-Christian life, and one that may
need unpacking for readers of Ephesians today, is "flesh"
(*sarx*) in 2:3. Although the term can be used by Paul in its
neutral or physiological sense of human corporeality (see,
for example, Rom 1:3; Gal 4:13-14; or 2 Cor 4:11), it more
often refers to humanity that is opposed to God. This latter
meaning is intended here in Ephesians. Although we usually think of the "passions of the flesh" as sins of carnality
that involve the body (for example, gluttony, drunkenness,
sexual sins), the list of the "works of the flesh" in Galatians
5:19-21 also includes many sins of disposition (envy, self-
ishness, party-spirit, and so on). Perhaps, the inclusion of
"mind" in Ephesians 2:3 is intended to clarify this point.
Those who appear morally upright in terms of their actions
can still be egocentric, living life for and by themselves
without being directed to God. Life in this present world-
age thus includes sins of carnality (the Greek word the RSV
translates "body" in 2:3 is also *sarx*) and the disposition.

Is life before salvation, as Paul has been characterizing
it in these opening verses of Ephesians 2. something that
humanity acquires (that is to say, is it a result of original
sin), or is it something for which we are responsible? The
phrase "by nature" has been taken to support a doctrine of
original sin, and elsewhere in the New Testament a similar
Greek construction seems to refer to something that comes
at birth (see Gal 2:15, which reads, "we who are Jews by
nature"). Andrew Lincoln concludes in his commentary:

> If original sin refers to the innate sinfulness of human
> nature inherited from Adam in consequence of the fall,
> then such a notion is not entirely alien to the thought of
> this verse when it speaks of the impossibility of human-
> ity of itself, in its natural condition, escaping God's
> wrath.[2]

He immediately qualifies this statement, however, by pointing out that this passage does not explicitly teach how this
condition is transmitted from parents to children, that sin
is of the essence of human nature, nor that humans are
absolved from responsibility for their actions. For Paul, sin
is always a disorder or abnormality in this world; and
throughout the section, words of volition and action are
used to describe the human plight that make it clear that
humans are not helpless victims without choice in the matter. We thus find in Ephesians a tension similar to the
thought of Romans 5:12-21 where humanity's natural condition as a result of Adam's disobedience is a fallen world,
but humans also share a solidarity with Adam by actively
disobeying God.

The contrast between this depiction of the human
condition and the following discussion (2:4-10) of God's
gracious actions in Christ underscore humanity's plight.
Left to their own device and efforts, humans cannot save
themselves and are deserving of God's wrath (the meaning
of the idiom "children of wrath"). Although the nature of
wrath is not further specified in 2:3, the reference is clearly
to God (cf. 5:6).

In other contexts, the Greek word *orgē* can mean anger
(see Mark 3:5; Jas 1:19-20, for example). Some think this is
an inappropiate emotion to ascribe to God. C. H. Dodd
notes, for example, that the verb form of "to be angry" is

never found in Paul and that of the eleven times the word "wrath" is used in Romans, only once is God's name specifically connected to it. He therefore concludes that in Paul wrath is an impersonal "law of retribution" placed by God in the universe so that evil consequences flow from sin.

Lincoln argues in his commentary, on the other hand, that wrath in Romans (as well as here in Ephesians) "refers to God's active judgment going forth against all forms of sin and evil and is evidence of his absolute holiness."[3] Crucial to this understanding of the wrath of God is that we see it as an expression of God's nature and not as a capricious act of anger against humanity.

God's actions toward humanity are described in 2:4-10. Having sketched humanity's plight in terms of death, disobedience, and condemnation, Paul vividly paints the contrast of what God has effected in Christ. Instead of wrath, we find mercy and grace. From death, there are resurrection and life in union with Christ. Instead of bondage to malevolent powers and willful disobedience, humanity is loved by God and created for good works.

As Paul describes the reversal of the Christian's position in these verses, a number of themes stand out. First, Paul's thought, as it was in the opening prayers of chapter 1, is radically theocentric. God is the subject of most of the verbs in the section. We may also find examples of the divine passive where God is assumed to be the one acting (see 2:5, 8, which read "by grace you have been saved"). God is the one who has acted not out of divine wrath, but out of mercy, love, and grace.

Mercy is a word with rich associations from the Old Testament. It usually translates the Hebrew word *hesed*, which is frequently used in the Old Testament to describe

God's steadfast love and covenant loyalty to Israel (see Exod 34:6, Ps 145:8, for example).

Love (the Greek word *agapē*) is the word used in the New Testament for God's love. It is an unconditional love that is given without regard to the worth or value of the persons or objects loved. Paul underlines the nature of this type of love in Ephesians 2:5 when he affirms that it was given "when we were dead through our trespasses."

The final word, "grace," also highlights the generous nature of God's gift. It was a common Greek word meaning "favor" or "gratitude," which Paul took over and became central to his gospel. It is used most frequently in his letters in contrast to law, and here the phrase "by grace" (2:4, 8) stresses the idea that salvation originates in God independent of any human source or action. The gospel comes as something outside of any human effort or striving to liberate humanity. As for the word's appearance in the New Testament, C. L. Mitton concludes, "There is no such thing as grace in the abstract, but only God acting graciously."[4]

The ultimate definition of God's grace is found in what God did in Christ to bring life and salvation to undeserving humanity. Thus, the second theme to strike the reader in this section is its Christocentricity. Salvation is possible through the believer's identification with Christ and participation in his life and resurrection. In the passage Paul uses a number of compound verbs formed with the Greek prefix *syn*, which can be translated "together with." Because Paul has described humanity's plight as death, Christians are thus made alive *together with* Christ (2:5), raised up *with* him and made to sit *with* him in the heavenlies (2:6).

The prepositional phrase "in Christ Jesus" at the end of 2:6 further underscores the centrality of Jesus in Paul's thought. The new life happens through the agency of Jesus, but the prepositional phrase also provides a clue to how salvation can be a present reality for the believer. By identifying with Christ and participating in his resurrection, Christians are freed from the bondage of death, sin, and hostile powers. They are transferred to a new sphere of power. Paul obviously recognized that his readers would be reading the letter with their feet firmly planted on the ground and still struggling (otherwise why would he bother with the ethical exhortations in the second half of the letter!), but he believed that Christ's death had fundamentally altered the power structures of the world. The old order of sin and death were defeated, and Christians' union with Christ meant that their existence was determined by this new sphere of power (cf. Eph 2:5-7 with similar ideas of participation in Rom 6:1-11).

Paul's emphasis on the present experience of salvation expressed in this idea of the believers sitting with Christ in the heavenlies and thus sharing his triumph over the powers of this age is a third theme that stands out in this section of the letter. Elsewhere in Paul the verb "to make alive" refers to a future bodily resurrection (see Rom 4:17; 8:11), but the tense in Ephesians 2:5 makes it clear that believers' experience of the resurrected life is before the end time. Most striking, perhaps, is Paul's use of the perfect passive tense of the verb "to save" in 2:5 and 2:8. This is the only time it appears in the letters in the perfect tense. More commonly in Paul's letters we find the future tense of "to save" (see Rom 5:9, 10; 10:9; 1 Cor 3:15; 5:5 for some examples) utilized to refer to the future, and ultimate, deliverance from the power of sin and death.

Paul also uses the verb in the present tense to refer to salvation as a present experience (see 1 Cor 1:18; 15:2 for examples) and even in the past tense in Romans 8:24 (in the Greek the verb is an aorist passive). This last example, however, qualifies the verb with the phrase "in hope." Grammatically, the perfect tense emphasizes the continuing effect of a past event, and, although unusual, fits in with the thought of Ephesians after the opening prayers of chapter 1. These prayers praised God for the blessings of salvation made available for believers.

It is best to think of salvation as a single process with different nuances or aspects of the process that can be highlighted. George Caird in his commentary argues that "salvation is always a past fact, a present experience, and a future hope, and it requires all three tenses for its adequate expression."[5] By using the perfect tense to underscore the present experience of salvation in Ephesians 2:5 and 8, Paul reinforces his readers' sense of identity as God's people. He also provides an encouraging word to those struggling with the hostile powers of this world-age. Through union with Christ in his resurrection, Christians share in his triumph over these powers.

Does this emphasis in Ephesians 2 on the present experience of salvation mean the tension we find elsewhere in Paul's thought between the "already" and "not yet" of Christian existence has been collapsed in a realized victory? I think not. Ephesians 2:7 suggests that Paul sees the new order as also having a future (see the reference to "in the coming ages"). Moreover, the prayers of thanksgiving and intercession in 1:15-22 and 3:14-21 as well as the ethical exhortations in the second half of the letter all contain an emphasis on the growth of the believers. Finally, the concluding call to stand firm in spiritual battle (6:13-20) helps put the letter's emphasis on the present experience of salvation in perspective and should "disabuse them [the readers] of any naive triumphalism."[6]

The final verses of this section (2:8-10) summarize Paul's understanding of the process of salvation by expanding the earlier exclamation that we have been saved by grace (2:5). These verses spell out God's initiative of grace, the human response of faith, and the practical goal of this process in terms of believers' daily lives. They spell it out, however, in ways that are distinctive from Paul's normal language. It is more typical in Paul to find the words grace, faith, and works used in conjunction with justification language instead of salvation language (see Rom 5:9, for example). Moreover, instead of speaking generally of works, Paul usually specifies "works of the law." Why the shift in language here in Ephesians?

Andrew Lincoln argues persuasively that Paul's use of phrases such as "works of the law" reflects a polemical context in which the apostle is in debate with Jewish Christianity about whether or not Gentile converts to Christianity need to keep the requirements of the Jewish law. The perspective in Ephesians, on the other hand, with the general terms salvation and works represents a broader perspective than this context of conflict. Instead of referring to specific Jewish legal requirements such as dietary laws, for example, "works" in Ephesians represent any human striving and are antithetical to the process of salvation.

The popularity of Ephesians 2:8-10 as a basic statement of Paul's gospel is perhaps explained by its movement to a more generalized statement about the process of salvation. Once the church developed a self-identity separate from Judaism so that the conflict between Gentiles and Jews in the church over the questions about keeping the law was a settled issue, the formulations of 2:8-10 became congenial to the ears of Christians. These verses speak to their own experiences of the grace and faith as companions in the process of salvation minus the conflict about obedience to Jewish legal requirements.

"Grace" emphasizes the divine initiative in the process. The phrase "by faith" expresses the human response to this initiative. Although faith can be used in the New Testament to refer to doctrines or the content of something believed (see Gal 2:23; Titus 1:1; or 1 Tim 5:8, for example), this human response is not intellectual assent to a set of propositions or doctrine, but one of trust and commitment to God.

The antecedent to the pronoun "this" in the second half of verse 8 is unclear, and commentators debate whether it refers to faith, grace, or the whole process? The consensus seems to be that the reference is to the whole process of salvation. There is thus no room in Paul's thought for the self-made person when it comes to one's relationship to God. Boasting and pride in all human strivings and achievements—be they fame, money, even orthodoxy—are included in the understanding of "works" and are excluded by Paul as forms of self-glorification that attempt to earn one merit before God. Such self-confidence in one's spiritual competence is antithetical to the trusting relationship of dependence found in faith.

The emphasis on God's initiative in the whole process of salvation that is so strongly underscored in these verses has been involved in misunderstandings throughout the church's history. One extreme has been to fall back into thinking that human effort contributes something to one's position before God. Early in the church's history, the issue was whether one needed to keep the Jewish law; but in later periods people, in the church preached the necessity for certain types of ascetic and ethical behavior, even orthodox beliefs, to gain a standing before God. Such additions to the gospel, however pious and well-meaning, ultimately raise questions about the adequacy of God's redeeming work in Christ Jesus. Ephesians 2:8-9 answers these questions with a resounding "NO." Andrew Lincoln aptly summarizes Paul's position with the dictum, "With grace as its ground and faith as its means, this salvation can have nothing to do with any notion of merit."[7]

The other extreme to be avoided is the danger of construing Paul's emphasis on God's gift in the process of salvation as an invitation to moral license. In other words, one should not believe that since Christians are saved by grace, it does not matter how one acts. If this position was the case, Christians would thus be free to indulge whatever passion and desire they may have (see Rom 6:1-2; 1 Cor 5-6 for examples of this type of misunderstanding and perversion of Paul's gospel). Paul is not against "good works," but against all attempts to make good works the source rather than the goal of the new relationship with God (see 2:10, for example, as Paul writes "for good works" rather than "by good works").

The same focus on God in the passage that we highlighted earlier is still operative in 2:10. This verse gives voice to Paul's concern for ethics. God is the one who has made Christians a new creation in Christ for the purpose of serving God and participating in his goodness and redemptive work in creation. The idea of God preparing these works beforehand makes it difficult for someone to construe these works as the grounds for pride and boasting. Rather, they are God's doing throughout.

This look back to God's pretemporal plans provides a link with the opening blessing in 1:4, but it does not result in ethical determinism. Christians still need to actively live out God's purposes in the world. This is the meaning of the verb "to walk," and it brings closure to the section by contrasting the former way of "walking" (how people live their lives and so express their being) in sin and death (2:1-2) with the changed lifestyle of being in Christ (2:10).

Throughout this opening section of chapter 2, the idea of identity has been an important theme, as it was in the prayers of Ephesians 1. The schema of once/now is employed in Paul's diagnosis of the human condition. He asks the readers to recall their pre-Christian past in bondage to sin and death and contrast that with the "now" of their new life in Christ. In describing the new life, Paul stresses in this section the present or realized aspects of his readers' experience of salvation. This serves to reinforce and strengthen their sense of identity as God's people. To avoid any hint of triumphalism in their perception of their experiences, however, Paul stresses that every different aspect of the process of salvation springs from God's gracious initiative—even the good works that are practiced and that make the contrast between once and now complete. The ethical implications of this new identity that results from God's redemptive action in Christ are unpacked in more detail in the second half of the letter. Here 2:11-22 utilizes the schema of then/now to spell out another facet of the readers' new identity: the reconciliation of Jew and Gentile in the church.

The New Humanity: Peace in Christ Jesus (2:11-22)

In 2:11 Paul's readers are explicitly identified as Gentiles, and their new identity means that they have a past vis-á-vis Israel and God. This past is now explored by means of the same contrast between then and now employed in 2:1-10. Although the thought shares the Trinitarian perspective found in the earlier prayers of chapter 1 (see 2:16, 18, which describe Christians as reconciled to God and having access to the Father through the Spirit), the focus in this passage is on Jesus and his role in God's redemptive work. The passage divides nicely into three units: 2:11-13 serves as the reminder that contrasts the readers' former alienation from Israel and God with the present experience of reconciliation; 2:14-18 is a hymn to Christ's work in effecting this reconciliation; and 2:19-22 expounds the nature of the church that results from Christ's work.

As Paul continues to address the theme of his readers' identity in 2:11-22, he does so not by describing their alienation from God on the basis of "trespasses and sins" (2:1), but by using religious symbols—circumcision, law, and temple—that divided Gentiles and Jews in the first century. The perspective is that of a Jewish-Christian who matter-of-factly describes the disadvantages of Gentiles vis-á-vis Jews (2:11-12). But the divisions and problems in the church that so excised Paul in Galatians are absent from Ephesians. The writer seems to look back to the past when these old divisions were overcome in Christ (see 2:14-16).

If there was a problem with the Ephesians, some commentators have suggested it was one of "ignorance of roots." Their salvation did not come about in a vacuum, but in history, and they have a place in that history. Jesus was Israel's Messiah, so that the contrast between the Ephesians' pre-Christian state (then) and the greatness of their salvation (now) is described in the context of Israel's history and privileges. This new identity involved incorporation into a new humanity that transcends the old categories of Gentile and Jew (see 2:15), however. There-fore, there is no question of either Gentile arrogance over against the Jews or of the church being a development in which Gentiles are joined together with Jews.

The term "uncircumcision" (2:11) was a word used by Jews to describe non-Jews. Since circumcision was the sign of Israel's covenant with God, the term developed a derog-atory sense. Those who were uncircumcised were deemed to be inferior because they were not in this covenant rela-tionship with God. While the writer of Ephesians utilizes this distinction between Jew and Gentile to describe the for-mer state of his readers, he also seems to distance himself from it when he characterizes circumcision as that "which is made in the flesh by hands." Elsewhere in the New Tes-tament the expression "to be made by hands" is employed to contrast old human physical acts or materials with a new spiritual order (see Acts 7:48; Heb 9:11, 24 for exam-ples). Here in Ephesians 2:11 the value of circumcision thus seems to be relativized. What is important to God is not outward physical appearance, but an inward disposition of faith. In Romans 2:28-29 Paul describes this "true circum-cision" as being of the heart.

What were the disadvantages of Ephesians' Gentile readers in their pre-Christian state over against Israel's position? These are enumerated in verse 12. Because Israel is God's chosen people (the focus of God's electing pur-poses in the Old Testament), Gentiles were alienated from God's promises. In this sense they were also separated from Christ in their pre-Christian state (which at first glance seems ro be a tautology, or repetition) because Jesus was Israel's promised Messiah.

The reference to being "without God" should not be construed as a reference to atheism. The ancient world knew of no atheism as we think of it today that denies belief in any God. In the first century there was a pantheon of different gods in the various religions for people to believe in. Rather, the Gentile readers may have had their pagan gods, but they were without the one true God—that is to say, the God who created the world, who saved Israel in the Exodus from Egypt and made a covenant with them, and who finally sent His son to die and be raised in order to reconcile humanity to God. The readers were thus without hope because without a relationship with this God and His son, they had no future.

All of these disadvantages that the Ephesians suffered in their previous state are overcome in Christ, however. Paul introduces the second half of the contrast ("now") in 2:13. Because the disadvantages of their pre-Christian state were described in terms of Israel's position, the language used to describe the reversal ("those once far off were brought near") probably draws upon a related linguistic pool. It is similar to language used to describe Jewish proselytism. That is to say, Gentiles who converted to Judaism were described in the Old Testament and later rabbinic interpretation as being brought near to promises of the community of Israel. If this is the allusion, however, the language of nearness is transformed by Paul because the Gentiles are not incorporated into Israel through Christ's work, but into a new humanity with access to God, as the rest of Ephesians 2 makes plain.

The change in the readers' condition is brought about "in the blood of Christ," which is Paul's way of referring to Jesus' death on the cross (see also 2:16). In a bold affirmation, Paul describes Jesus as "our peace" (2:14). Although we often define peace today as the stopping of war and absence of hostilities, it is a word rooted in the Old Testament that means much more than this. "Peace" (*shalom*) denotes well-being and security, even salvation, and is often viewed as God's gift. Here it is connected to Jesus' person and is not based upon any human effort.

This peace has both a vertical and a horizontal dimension. The vertical dimension is expressed in the reconciliation between humans and God (2:16, 18; cf. Rom 5:1). The horizontal or social implications of this peace mean that enmities between humans—Jew and Gentile in this case—are overcome in Jesus' death. His work on the cross and nothing else—shared political views or social-economic standing, for example—creates the new humanity we know as the church.

In this section Paul uses Jesus' death to reconfigure the Jewish religious symbols of law and temple. For the Jewish people these were God's gifts and a part of their distinctive claim as God's chosen people. They had become twisted, however, when they were used to separate people and build a "dividing wall of hostility" (2:14). The imagery used here is complex, and commentators generally offer two possible explanations to the wall between Jew and Gentile.

One explanation is based on the physical layout of the Jerusalem temple that had a wall dividing the outer court of the Gentiles from the inner courts. Archaeologists have found an inscription on one of the pillars of the temple that reads "No man of another race is to enter within the fence and enclosure. Whoever is caught will have only himself to thank for the death which follows." Since the temple was viewed as God's special dwelling place, Gentiles were denied the access to God that law-abiding Jews enjoyed. The physical layout of the temple thus symbolized both a wall between different peoples as well as a wall between God and humans. Paul claims that this alienation and hostility have been brought to an end through Jesus' death.

A second explanation suggested for the imagery of a dividing wall identifies the fence as the Mosaic law and subsequent scribal interpretations of it. In the *Letter to Aristeas* (a second-century B.C. Jewish document), the Law, and the oral traditions that grew up interpreting it, is described as a fence that separates and protects the Jewish people from the impurities of the Gentiles. Christ thus ends the hostility that such an approach to the Law creates by "abolishing in his flesh the law of commandments and ordinances" (2:15). The force of Paul's thought seems to be that any claim to special status or access to God that the law or temple offered to Jews has been ended in Christ and is now granted as a free gift to all people (see 2:17-18). The allusion to Isaiah 57:19 in 2:17 implies that Israel was also alienated from God before Christ's death. Jesus' death on the cross was the creative force that reconciled hostile humanity both to God and to each other.

In this passage we find the theme of discontinuity between the church and Israel more heavily stressed than in some other letters of Paul. In Romans 3:31, for example, Paul denies abolishing the law. We should be careful today when we read about the abolishment of the law that we do not read this assertion in an antinomian way. (The Greek word usually translated "law" is *nomos*, so that is to say, in a way that is against the law.) Later in Ephesians (6:2), for example, Paul quotes one of the Ten Commandments to support his ethical advice to his readers. Paul is still concerned with morality or ethics, and the law can still serve as a source for formulating these guidelines. What appears to be abolished are the law's power and condemnation as characteristic of the old order, which was at enmity with

God. A new order and power have been ushered in through the creative force of Jesus' death.

In Ephesians this new humanity in Christ that we know as the church transcends older categories such as Jew and Gentile and does not simply merge the two. Paul here does not show the same concern for Israel or the law that we find in places such as Romans 9–11. Christian history with its accounts of expulsion, forced conversion, and persecution of Jews bears witness to how the church has taken this idea in Ephesians of the church as a new creation and denied Israel any continuing validity as a people. After the Holocaust, we need to bear witness in repentance and love in our actions. In terms of Jewish-Christian dialogue, Ephesians' vision of reconciliation in the church in which the alienation and enmity of Paul's readers in their pre-Christian state were overcome by God offers hope that God's grace and reconciliation can be experienced by others.

The new community created by Jesus' death is described in 2:19-22 with a return to the imagery of the temple. The temple was viewed by the Jewish people as God's special dwelling place on the earth, but now the focus of God's dwelling place is the new humanity created by Jesus (2:22). Because of the church's connection with Jesus the cornerstone and the presence of the Holy Spirit, it, and not the Jerusalem temple, becomes the special link between heaven and earth. This community is one in which not only the hostility between God and humanity has been overcome, but also one in which reconciliation between people is accomplished. The church should be a visible sign of the harmony in the world that God is working toward in Christ Jesus.

In 2:19 this harmony is described as a unity between Gentile and Jew. Gentiles are no longer second-class citizens, but full and equal participants in the new community. The unity in which ethnic distinctions are overcome is similar to what is expressed in Galatians 3:28 when Paul writes that "there is neither Jew nor Greek, there is neither slave nor free, there is neither male nor female; for you are all one in Christ Jesus."

In using building imagery, Paul presents the foundation of this community as "the apostles and prophets" (2:20). Who are these people? Most likely, early Christian leaders. Ordinarily, we think of apostles as those who were the original followers of Jesus (see Acts 1) or other messengers and eyewitnesses of the resurrection (see Rom 16:7; 1 Cor 7–9, for example). The term "prophets" is probably not a reference to figures from the Old Testament, but would designate early Christian preachers who exercised the gift of prophecy (see Rom 12:6; 1 Cor 11, 14 for discussions of this gift).

The perspective here is slightly different from 1 Corinthians 3:10-11 where Paul asserts that the only foundation for the church is Jesus Christ. In Ephesians 2, however, Christ is the "cornerstone." That is to say, he is the keystone in the foundation from which all other stones take their bearing. Christ's pivotal role in the formation and life of the church is thus still highlighted. Apostles and prophets can be said to be a part of this foundation because of their ministry of the word. This ministry proclaims the gospel and hands on the traditions about Christ (including their "literary deposits" in what we know as the New Testament), thus making it possible for others to be joined to this community.

Unlike the third chapter of 1 Corinthians, the building and temple imagery used in Ephesians have the universal church in view. God's presence in the Spirit is focused not just in individuals, not just in local congregations, but in the universal church. Since the resurrected Jesus as the cornerstone of the community is a living Lord, the building is living and growing as "the holy temple in the Lord" (2:21). Church growth is thus defined not in terms of buildings and numbers; nor is holiness merely an individual concern. Rather, church growth and holiness are a continuous process that have a corporate context. Paul mixes his metaphors to a certain extent in 2:21-22 when he portrays the temple as a living and growing organism in which Christians are built into a fit sanctuary for God's presence. For Christians today this means that church growth should not be measured simply in quantitative terms of numbers, but also in qualitative terms moving toward a goal of holiness so that our daily lives may be set apart in service (cf. Rom 12:1-2).

Conclusion

We argued in the previous chapter that Paul uses praise and prayer in Ephesians 1 to help reinforce the identity of his readers. Through praise for what God has accomplished in Christ Jesus, Paul constructs a world and establishes the Ephesians' identity in it. Ephesians 2 still addresses the issue of identity, but it uses the language of remembrance and recall.

Paul invites the Ephesians to remember their pre-Christian past and contrasts that state with their Christian present. Their past was characterized by death and bondage. Their present involves life and is determined by grace. In their past they were alienated both from God and from Israel. In their present these hostilities are overcome as Jew and Gentile are reconciled in the church through Christ's work. The contrast between once and now operative throughout this chapter of Ephesians serves to remind the readers of their place in the new humanity that God is creating as well as helping to sustain them.

Because Ephesians emphasizes the present experience of salvation for believers and the greatness of God's work in contrast to the readers' pre-Christian condition, the letter has sometimes been accused of fostering a Christian triumphalism. We must be careful as we read Ephesians not to fall into attitudes of arrogance, self-satisfaction, or collective pride for the privileges God has gifted us with. An opposite, and more appropriate, response is one of gratitude and humility for all that God has done. We should not take the privileges of salvation for granted.

With such an attitude, Ephesians challenges Christians to live up to the identity and calling God has given us. The unity of the church is not just limited to a unity between Jewish Christian and Gentile Christian in the first century. The picture of the church in Ephesians calls Christians of every age to overcome any division of race, nationality, economics, or social standing. Anything less is a denial of the nature of the church as a reconciled and reconciling body. As we shall see, Paul develops these ideas in more detail later in the letter.

Questions for Reflection

1. In what ways does Paul use the then/now schema to remind the Ephesians of the contrast between their pre-Christian condition and their Christian existence? What terms would you use in such a scheme to describe your life?

2. Describe the past, present, and future aspects of the process of salvation in Paul's thought.

3. How can faith be both a gift from God and a human response? What is the relationship between grace and good works in Ephesians 2?

4. What divisions in the church today need to be overcome if the church is to reach the ideal of the new humanity created by Christ's death?

5. What perspectives can Ephesians contribute to issues raised by a special mission to the Jewish people or the nature of Jewish-Christian dialogue?

Notes

[1]C. K. Barrett, *Paul: An Introduction to His Thought* (Louisville: Westminster/John Knox, 1994) 61.

[2]Andrew T. Lincoln, *Ephesians*, Word Biblical Commentary, 42 (Waco TX: Word, 1990) 99.

[3]Ibid., 98.

[4]C. L. Mitton, *Ephesians*, New Century Bible (Grand Rapids MI: Eerdmans, 1973) 92.

[5]George B. Caird, *Paul's Letters from Prison*, The Clarendon Bible (Oxford: Oxford University Press, 1976) 21.

[6]A. T. Lincoln and A. J. M. Wedderburn, *The Theology of the Later Pauline Letters* (Cambridge: Cambridge University Press, 1993) 116.

[7]Lincoln, *Ephesians*, 118.

Chapter 3

Paul's Ministry of
Revelation and Prayer for the Church

Ephesians 3:1-21

The Church will become more what it ought to be as it experiences more of the one who mediates God's purposes in salvation, more of Christ's presence through the Spirit, and more of his all-embracing love that surpasses knowledge.
—Andrew T. Lincoln

For many Christians today, the church almost seems to be an optional part of their existence. Polls show that while the percentage of Americans professing religious beliefs remains very high, attendance and participation in churches are on the decline. In our glorification of the individual, religion has become a personal and private matter. The attitude of many is that Christian community can be experienced as easily through the television as it can through the fellowship of other believers.

Such an attitude is at odds with the perspective of Ephesians where the church and its role in God's purposes come to the forefront. We have seen how Paul in the first two chapters of Ephesians has reminded and reinforced his readers' identity through the language of worship and remembrance. Part of the new identity they have as Christians is that they are in the church—the body of Christ and Christ's fullness (1:23), God's family (2:19), and a new temple that they are being built into as the bricks (2:20-22). When Paul uses these different images in Ephesians for the church, he has in view the church in its totality, or what we often call the universal church. As he discusses his readers' identity and how they came to be who they are as the church, however, he reminds them of their indebtedness to the apostle Paul.

The description of the new humanity as one in which Jew and Gentile are united (2:11-22) leads to a digression (3:1-13) that underscores the centrality of Paul's apostolic ministry in the revelation of the mystery of God's purposes. It also affirms the church's role in the mystery. In this digression the church is not only the context of revelation, it is also part of the content of the mystery. Such an exalted idea of the church's role in God's plans leads into a prayer for the church's growth and maturity (3:14-21) because Paul realizes that if the church is going to fulfill its function, "God is going to have to help it in a big way."[1]

Paul's Ministry of
Revelation and Reconciliation
(3:1-13)

Paul's statement about the unity of the church in the end of chapter 2 spurs a thought that is not completed until the intercessory prayer of 3:14 (3:1 and 3:14 both begin "for this reason"). The identification of the person praying as "Paul, a prisoner for Christ Jesus on behalf of you Gentiles" leads to a digression about Paul's ministry. The digression of 3:2-13 is primarily composed of two long sentences in Greek (3:2-7, 8-12) that provide parallel statements about the mystery of the gospel. The first sentence highlights Paul's apostolic ministry as the primary mediator of the revelation of the mystery that Gentiles and Jews are equal participants or members in the new humanity God has created in the Christ. The second sentence highlights the church's role in mediating this mystery to hostile spiritual powers.

Modern readers of Ephesians are confronted with the question of authorship when they read this section. Do these words read like Paul talking about himself or like the description by a later admirer, perhaps even a disciple, of a beloved leader? Those who accept Pauline authorship of the epistle point out that the author is explicitly identified as Paul (3:1) and the section has a concentration of first person pronouns throughout.

Proponents of pseudonymous authorship, however, argue that these are common literary devices of pseudonymity. Does the wording of 3:2 imply a lack of knowledge or familiarity between readers and Paul? Although Paul can boast about his apostleship (see 2 Cor 10-13, for example), it is usually when he was attacked. Would Paul have talked about his insight into the mystery of Christ as he does in Ephesians 3:4 without any apparent provocation?

Finally, this passage has close parallels with Colossians 1:23-28. Both use a similar vocabulary and develop a similar sequence of themes. For example, both introduce Paul, mention his suffering, discuss the apostolic office, reveal the content of the mystery of God, and proclaim that mystery. Are these similarities best explained by the two letters being written by the same man at roughly the same time, or did another person take Colossians to adapt freely and creatively when writing Ephesians?

The content of this review of Paul's apostleship in Ephesians 3 is primarily well-known, general aspects of Paul's biography: he was an apostle to the Gentiles, whose calling was dependent on grace, the recipient of a special revelation, and imprisoned and suffering for his part in bringing the gospel to the Gentiles. Some of these elements, however, deserve further comment.

First, this passage underscores that the readers are Pauline Christians. They are indebted to the apostle either because of his work directly with them (if we accept Pauline authorship of the letter) or because as Gentile readers Paul's mission made possible the gospel being proclaimed outside Judaism. Perhaps more fundamentally, however, this passage suggests that the readers owe their new identity as Christians to God's grace for Paul's ministry, which is grounded in God's gift and is a stewardship of that grace (see 3:2, 7-8).

Although Ephesians 3 does not develop this idea extensively, we can view Paul's life as a paradigm of divine grace; one who violently opposed the gospel and persecuted the church is called by God to proclaim the gospel he once tried to destroy (cf. Gal 1:10-17). In that experience on the road to Damascus, Paul experienced the power of God that overcame the bondage of the old age and incorporated him into the new humanity in Christ. God's gift of grace to Paul was unmerited and undeserved, coming to "the very least of all the saints." Out of such an experience of grace and power Paul now preaches the gospel of "the unsearchable riches of Christ" (3:8). His preaching does not arise from some theoretical, intellectual knowledge, but from the lived experience of God's grace.

A second element to note in the depiction of Paul's ministry in Ephesians 3 is that Paul is minister and theologian of the church. He does not sit in an ivory tower in front of a computer writing theological books that few will read! For Paul, to be a steward of God's grace means that he is proclaiming the gospel, working to make all see God's mystery that had been hidden but is now revealed. Although Paul might have been a primary vehicle through which God's grace was proclaimed to the Gentiles, he was not alone. Ephesians places Paul squarely in the center of the church with the "holy apostles and prophets by the Spirit" (3:5).

Another sense in which Paul is minister and theologian of the church, however, is seen in how the focus of God's mystery is centered on the church in Ephesians 3. The church is the context for the revelation of God's mystery. The schema of past/present, which structures so much of Paul's thinking in the first two chapters of Ephesians, is also at work in 3:4-5. The "mystery of Christ" had not been made known in the past, but has been known now after the death and resurrection of Christ in the church. The Spirit made the revelation known to "holy apostles and prophets," who earlier have been identified as the foundation of the new community (see 2:20).

What is the mystery of Christ here in Ephesians? The focus is again on the church, not simply as the context of revelation but also as the content of the revelation of the mystery. This mystery (notice that Paul uses the singular form of the noun rather than the plural) is that Gentiles are joint heirs and members of the church (3:6). In this verse we find a concentration of verbs with the prefix *syn*. This is similar to the concentration of compound verbs in 2:5-6 where Paul stresses the believers' identification and participation in Christ's death and resurrection. Here the point seems to be that in Christ the Gentiles have a full and equal share in the promises of salvation. Jew and Gentile alike are equal participants, not in Israel but in the new humanity God has created.

A third element to note in this depiction of Paul's ministry and the church is that the church has cosmic significance in God's plans (3:9-10). Earlier the mystery has been made known to Paul (3:3) and to apostles and

prophets (3:5). Now the church makes known the "mani-
fold wisdom of God" (which here seems to function as the
equivalent of the "mystery" mentioned earlier; cf. 1 Cor
2:6-8 where "wisdom" and "mystery" are also linked) to
cosmic "principalities and powers." These were nonhuman,
angelic and demonic figures. The first-century worldview
may seem strange to many twentieth-century readers, but
for Paul's readers, these spiritual forces were hostile agen-
cies with power in the world (cf. Eph 6:12). Paul's perspective is that on this side of Easter, the church's existence
proclaims to these malevolent powers that their rule has
ended in Christ. Instead, Christians have bold and confi-
dent access to God through Jesus (3:12).

We find the same theocentric perspective in these
verses that we have commented on throughout our discussion of Ephesians. The wisdom of God seems to refer to
God's general, hidden plan for the world. It has been hidden not only through the ages, but "in God" (3:9). Now in
Jesus, God's purposes that were hidden in His nature are
realized. Paul does not spell out here how the church
makes this purpose known. Some commentators suggest it
is through its proclamation (see 3:8), while others suggest
it is through its worship. Andrew Lincoln argues that the
church makes known God's purposes simply through its
existence as the new humanity in Christ. The unity of the
church that God has brought into being is part of the larger
harmony that God is working toward with the universe to
bring all things together in subjection to Christ (see Eph
1:9-10 where Paul also uses the word "mystery" in his
opening eulogy). By overcoming the major first-century
division between Jew and Gentile, "the Church reveals
God's secret in action and heralds to the hostile heavenly
powers the overcoming of cosmic divisions with their

defeat."[2] The church, in short, is the one place that the world can see reconciliation as a reality.

This digression on Paul's ministry closes as it began with an emphasis on the link between Paul and the readers (the same Greek preposition *hyper*, meaning "for" or "on behalf of" is used in 3:1, 13). The author of Ephesians wants to underscore that the Ephesians' identity as Christians and their place in the church within the cosmic drama is integrally linked with Paul's ministry. The mention in both places of Paul's imprisonment and suffering reminds us that Paul's apostleship did not lead to an easy life of wealth and riches for him. Instead of a gospel of glory so often preached today in our country, promising wealth and success to the religious, Paul's life reminds us that obedience to Christ can be costly (although it must be admitted that Ephesians does not develop a profound theology of the cross like we find in other New Testament documents). In Ephesians 3:13 Paul's apostolic suffering is for the benefit of the readers, and they are reminded of it as a way of encouragement. Given the crucial role the church plays in God's plan, however, the readers are in need of more than encouragement. Paul is thus moved to offer an intercessory prayer for his readers beginning with 3:14.

Paul's Prayer for Depth
A Church Rooted in Love
(3:14-21)

The first half of Ephesians, which can be characterized as a prayerful meditation of God's work in the world and the church, ends as it began—with prayer. This section is one long sentence in Greek, but it can be structured into three parts: (1) verses 14-15 are the introduction to the prayer, (2) verses 16-19 function as the intercessory prayer itself, and (3) verses 19-20 contain a concluding doxology. The actual content of the prayer can also be divided into three main requests with each request introduced with the Greek word *hina* ("in order that"). Paul prays that the Ephesians may be strengthened (3:16), empowered (3:18), and filled (3:19b). Other requests in the prayer flesh out in different terms what these major requests mean.

Some commentators have suggested that the emphases in the intercessions reflect what Paul perceived to be the needs of his readers. Both here and in the earlier prayer of 1:15-23 we find requests for strength and power (1:19; 3:16, 18). Evidently Paul saw the need for vigorous Christians who could stand firm against the hostile spiritual powers (see 6:10-20). In both prayers, knowledge is connected to this empowering (1:17-18; 3:18-19). The issue of his readers' identity becomes important at this point because the knowledge of who they are and what God has done for them will help strengthen them for the church's fulfillment of its appointed role.

Paul's prayer is not for an abstract, arid, intellectual knowledge, however, detached from experience. Rather, it is an experiential knowledge rooted in the life-giving, life-transforming power of the Spirit. Experiential and intellectual knowledge of God's love should thus mutually sustain each other. One new emphasis in this second prayer, as we shall see, is Paul's request that the readers be rooted and grounded in love (3:17). Such a prayer may reflect a concern about instability in his readers, so Paul prays that they may grow in maturity.

The prayer introduction (3:14) begins with the same words, "for this reason," that Paul started with in 3:1.

Although he does not specify the nature of the reason he is moved to pray, we can conjecture that it continues his thought about the nature of the new humanity of Jew and Gentile (2:11-22)—that is to say, the church—and its role in God's purposes (3:2-13). Whatever the reason, however, we should note that Paul saw value in intercessory prayer and seems to think it a part of his responsibility toward others. Contemporary questions about whether God listens or what prayer accomplishes are absent from Paul's actions. His theology made a place for prayer and should challenge us both individually and corporately as the church to do likewise. Prayers are too often the first thing cut in many Baptist worship services as the order of service fills with other activities and emphases.

Although the posture of prayer adopted by Paul, "to bow my knees," may seem quite normal to contemporary readers of Ephesians, this was not the normal stance for Jews and early Christians praying in the first century. Typically, the petitioner would stand (see Luke 18:11, 13, for example). In antiquity, to bow the knees was an act of servility or worship, appropriate for submission before a king or god. We should not see intercessory prayer and worship as unconnected activities, however. The posture adopted by Paul should be understood as an act of reverence for the God to whom one prays.

The God to whom Paul prays is identified as "the Father." One is reminded of Jesus' address to God as *Abba*, the Aramaic word for father that denotes familial love and respect. Some Greek manuscripts expand further the idea of father with the words "of our Lord Jesus Christ" (see the King James Version for an English translation that follows these manuscripts), but the best Greek manuscripts omit these words. To follow the shorter reading here, however, is not to imply that Paul did not see God as the father of Jesus (in a unique way). It also does not mean that Paul did not understand God to be father for Christians because of what Jesus has accomplished (see Rom 8:15-17; Gal 4:4-7, for example).

Paul does expand on the idea of God the Father, however, in Ephesians 3:15 through a play on words that may not be as obvious in English as it is in Greek. The Greek word for "father" used in 3:15 is *patēr*, which is related to the word for "family" (*patria*) in 3:16. God is thus identified as the father of "every family in heaven" (groupings or classes of angels and spirits, an idea found in some Jewish literature) and "on earth" (human family groupings). In short, Paul sets God's fatherhood "in the context of creation and of the cosmos."[3] Such a view is consistent with the perspective we have found elsewhere in Ephesians where both Christ and the church also have cosmic significance. In Ephesians, God is Father not only as redeemer but also as creator. Because Paul is asking for big requests for his readers, he prays to a big God!

The intercessory prayer requests begin in 3:16 and ask God to provide for the readers out of "the riches of his glory." The idea of God's riches or wealth is a popular theme in Ephesians, and this prayer is addressed to the one upon whom the entire cosmos is dependent. This is some wealth! God's glory would entail not only his radiance, but, more importantly, also his power.

The first request is that the Ephesians might be strengthened. We see in this request the piling up of synonymous words so typical of the style of Ephesians ("to be strengthened with power"). This power that is available to Christians is the same power that raised Christ from the dead (1:19). It is mediated to Christians through "his

Spirit," which is clearly a reference to the Holy Spirit. The third person of the Trinity became the means by which God is present with His people after Jesus' death and resurrection (see John 14:15-17, 25-26, for example).

What is the "inner man" where this strengthening takes place? The anthropology seems dualistic in nature, and the reference would be to a person's center of being. Similar descriptions of humans are found in 2 Corinthians 4:16 and Romans 7:22. In the passage from 2 Corinthians the inner man is the part of a person that is being renewed. The immediate context there implies that a person's inner nature may be equivalent to the heart (2 Cor 4:6), although in Romans 12:2 it is the mind that is being renewed. It is interesting to note that we find a similar cluster of concepts here in Ephesians 3 to describe God's transforming and empowering work in Christians. Wherever we locate this "inner man," however, the implication of the prayer is that it is a place that may not be visible but is open and susceptible to God's work. Here the energizing work of the Holy Spirit can produce effective Christians.

Ephesians 3:17 elaborates on this initial request by spelling out in different terms how God can strengthen the Christian with power. The first parallel statement prays for "Christ to dwell in your hearts through faith." Elsewhere Paul can use the expression "in Christ" and "in the Spirit" interchangeably (see Rom 8:1-17, for example, especially, vv. 9, 11, which speak of the Spirit dwelling in believers). In this request Christ seems to be the functional equivalent to Spirit in the preceding prayer. Through the Spirit's presence the risen Christ is present and active in the lives of Christians. The prayer is not for a one-time experience, however, but for Christ's continuing presence. It asks that he take up residence in a person's heart through faith.

Although today we often think of the heart as the organ of emotion, in the Old Testament in the anthropology of the Hebrews, the heart was the center for willing and thinking. The prayer, in short, asks that Christians have Christ-centered and Christ-controlled lives.

Paul mixes his metaphors in the second parallel request of Ephesians 3:17 when he prays for the Ephesians to be "rooted and grounded in love." He uses images drawn from horticulture and architecture. When a plant is "rooted," its root system goes deep into the soil to draw up the nutrients and water necessary to live and grow. Buildings are "grounded" when their foundations are sunk deep into the earth to provide the necessary support for the structure. Jesus used both metaphors in parables.

In the parable of the Sower (Matt 13:1-9 and parallels), some seed fell on rocky ground, and although it grew, the plants were not rooted and thus were unable to endure the withering sun and drought. Other seeds, however, fell on good ground, took root, and produced a bountiful crop. In the parable of the Two Builders that ends the Sermon on the Mount (Matt 7:24-27), one builder built his house with an inadequate foundation on sand so that it could not withstand the onslaught of wind and weather. The wise builder, however, grounded his house on rock so that it would stand against the flood.

In Jesus' parables and in Ephesians, the metaphors work together to convey the idea that Christians have a depth dimension to their lives. If they are to grow, they must be rooted. If they are to stand, they must have a firm foundation.

In Ephesians 3:17 the soil and foundation in which Christians are to be planted and grounded is simply identified as love. Commentators debate whether this love is

God's love that has been expressed through Christ or the Christian's love. Andrew Lincoln warns against making too sharp a distinction between the two alternatives here in Ephesians. Certainly God's self-giving love in Christ provides the basis for Christian existence, but it also calls and empowers believers to love others in an unconditional way (see 1 Cor 13, for example).

The second major request of the intercessory prayer concerns the readers' knowledge (3:18-19a). This request is filled with the rhetorical flourishes we find elsewhere in Ephesians and gives voice to the paradoxes so characteristic of religious experience. Paul prays that as the Ephesians are strengthened, they may be able to know the incomprehensible love of Christ. It is a knowledge that is shared in fellowship with the whole church ("the saints" in 3:18 is a reference to all Christians), and thus is not a matter of individual ability, IQ, or level of education.

The request also contains no contrast between an individual's love and knowledge, nor does it put down knowledge. Rather, Christ's love is so vast and all-embracing (the meaning of the four dimensions mentioned in 3:18b; compare this with the description of God's love in Rom 8:35-39) that humans are unable to comprehend it totally. It retains a character of mystery, and yet the prayer is that the Ephesians may know such a love. George Caird has argued that in this mystery "the attempt to know the unknowable is a paradox which is at the heart of all true religion."[4]

The final request in Ephesians 3:19b with its request for the readers to "be filled with all the fullness of God" brings the intercession to a bold climax. It is climactic not only because it moves from the incomprehensible love of Christ to God, but because of its breathtaking boldness. It asks that believers be filled up with the very fullness of God.

Whatever their inadequacies, shortcomings, or insecurities, these can be compensated for by God.

Perhaps after working up to such a climax, Paul breaks forth with the only appropriate response—praise. He concludes his prayer with a doxology (3:21-21). I would like to draw attention to two items in the doxology. First, we notice that Paul has again shifted pronouns in the doxology to the first person plural (3:20). Petitioner and recipients are thus drawn together in making the prayers and the praise their own.

Second, the doxology is striking in the way in which it parallels the church and Christ (3:21). Since the church has been identified as the focus of God's presence and rule on earth (1:22-23; 2:22), it is also the place of God's glorification. The parallel does not mean that church and Christ are equal, for the church's role as the locus for God's glorification is dependent upon Christ's work, dependent upon Christians being incorporated into Christ's body. And yet, as the only doxology in the New Testament to include the church, it gives the church a significant role in God's purposes.

Andrew Lincoln has argued in one of his studies of Ephesians that "Christian existence does not merely consist of ethical activities. It has a depth dimension to it."[5] This intercessory prayer of Paul's in Ephesians gives expression to the apostle's concern for this depth dimension in his readers. It is a prayer for Christian maturity and growth. It encourages the Ephesians to cultivate an ongoing, personal relationship with Christ. In many ways, the different requests all ask for the same thing: to be Christ-centered, controlled, and powered. This is the identity God has called and created for the new humanity in Christ.

In the second half of the letter Paul will move to spell out some implications for living out the mandates of this new life. This closing prayer in the first half of the letter provides a nice transition to the sorts of ethical and moral advice found in the second half because the theological affirmations of the readers' new identity, appropriated and reinforced through worship and prayer, function as the ground and foundation out of which Christian ethical character springs. Ethical action should be seen as the grateful response to what God has accomplished in Christ.

Questions for Reflection

1. What is the mystery of Christ that Paul talks about in Ephesians 3? What role did Paul's ministry have in making known this mystery? What role does the church have in the revelation of the mystery?
2. What is Paul's prayer for the church?
3. How do you experience or know the incomprehensible love and power of God in your life? What might it mean to be filled with the fullness of God?
4. In what ways or activities might the church bring glory to God?

Notes

[1]Andrew T. Lincoln, *Ephesians*, Word Biblical Commentary, 42 (Waco TX: Word, 1990) 218.

[2]Ibid., 187.

[3]Ibid., 203.

[4]George B. Caird, *Paul's Letters from Prison*, The Clarendon Bible (Oxford: Oxford University Press, 1976) 70.

[5]Lincoln, 120.

Chapter 4

Living the New Life

Ephesians 4:1–5:20

My father had an aphorism, "character is how you behave when no one is looking." . . . Are we ever in a situation when "no one is looking?" . . . I suppose I would have my father's aphorism assert that character is how you behave in response to the company you keep, seen and unseen.

—Robert Coles

In his book *The Spiritual Life of Children*, Harvard psychologist and Pulitzer prize-winning author Robert Coles describes a conversation he had with a small girl of eight years old in 1962 during the integration of public schools in North Carolina. The young girl was entering school alone, surrounded by people who were screaming at her, when the little girl told Coles, "Suddenly I saw God smiling, and I smiled back." A woman standing near the school door shouted at her, "Hey you little nigger, what are you smiling at?" The girl continued her story to Coles. "I looked right at her face, and I said, 'At God.' Then she looked up at the sky, then she looked at me, and she didn't call me any more names."[1]

Perhaps that dialogue became a moment of revelation for the woman harassing the little girl. Perhaps in that moment she recognized the common bond of humanity between herself and another person created in the image of God. Perhaps the woman was a Christian and in that moment realized that her identity in the new humanity created in Christ meant that her behavior should exhibit the love God had extended to her. Perhaps.

For Paul writing Ephesians, identity and behavior are closely linked. Although most of Paul's letters have a section of moral exhortation and ethical advice, this section is expanded to comprise the second half of Ephesians (chaps 4–6). The moral exhortations are closely linked, however, to the theological realities expounded in the first half of the letter in the language of worship, prayer, and remembrance. The emphasis there on the present experience of salvation and the realized victory of Jesus over hostile powers of the old age does not imply that Christians have no further struggle (see 6:10-20) or an easy life without moral standards.

If Jesus had been a country-western singer, he might have told his disciples in the Sermon on the Mount, "I never promised you a rose garden!" The perspective of Paul in Ephesians is that the gift of the new life he has described in the first half of Ephesians has requirements that spring forth from the gift. They are not conditions to receiving the gift, but they are grateful responses to the gift. In short, Paul appeals for behavior that is consistent with the new identity God has given Christians. For this reason Paul uses "therefore" to begin the section of exhortation because the ethical appeals presuppose and are based on all that has been said in the first three chapters.

The appeal in 4:1 is "to lead a life worthy of the calling to which you have been called." God's gracious initiative in Christ Jesus not only entails blessings, it also involves responsibilities. The exhortation for behavior consistent with identity is true not only for individuals (see 4:23-24), it also applies to the church as a whole (see 4:15-16). The Greek verb *peripateo*, "to walk," used in 4:1 appears frequently throughout this second half of Ephesians (4:1, 17; 5:2, 8, 15) and underscores something of Paul's concern in this section for the Ephesians. To use a contemporary cliché, he wants them "to walk the walk and not just talk the talk." In this half of Ephesians, we find the vision of the first half of the letter being directed to practical, down-to-earth concerns of living the new life in the world.

Maintaining the Unity of the Reconciled Church (4:1-16)

Since earlier in the letter Paul identified the mystery of Christ as the one church in which Jew and Gentile lived in harmony as equal and essential members, it is not surprising to find Paul addressing the church's unity as the first topic in the exhortation. In this section Paul first urges conduct that will preserve the unity (4:1-3), which then leads to a series of seven assertions about the fundamental unities that undergird the church's existence (4:4-6). He then turns to the diversity of gifts within the church's unity that allows the church to grow in maturity and love (4:7-16).

The unity of the church is not simply a divine gift rooted in God's gracious actions. It is also something that is to be maintained and cultivated by Christians (4:3). Paul thus lists four qualities or attitudes that will contribute to the unity of the church: humility, meekness, patience, and forebearance in love. Every one of these qualities is characterized by the absence of self-assertion and self-aggrandizement. Each quality springs from an awareness that the Christian's new life is dependent upon God's grace and so recognizes the value and worth of the lives of fellow believers.

These initial appeals to unity lead not to more appeals, but to a series of acclamations that assert the fundamental unities of the church (4:4-6). Most commentators think that Paul has taken over traditional confessional material associated with baptism in these assertions. The assertions form three couplets that culminate with a final affirmation of monotheism. The one God who is both transcendent and immanent in all is the source and ground of unity as the universal Father. Some have seen in these affirmations the genesis of a basic Trinitarian belief with the mention of one God the Father, one Lord, and one Spirit. It is nothing like the developed doctrine of later creeds, however, and the emphasis in the passage falls more on one body, one Lord, and one God rather than on the three persons of the Trinity. Paul moves from the oneness of the church to the oneness of its Lord and the oneness of its God.

In these affirmations of unity, Paul connects to ideas found in the first half of the letter. The one body is the church made up of Jews and Gentiles (2:16; 3:6). The one Spirit is the Holy Spirit at work in the body, giving access to the Father (1:13; 2:18). Paul prayed in his first intercessory prayer (1:18) that Christians might grow in the hope that God called them. Earlier Paul had described the culmination of salvation as the summing up and uniting of all things in Christ (1:9-10). Andrew Lincoln thus concludes that the one hope in 4:4 refers not to an individual and private hope, but to a "corporate and public one" of a unified and reconciled world. Because hope draws people forward into the future, it can direct and shape behavior. Affirming one hope of the nature is thus appropriate when urging Christians to maintain unity.

The one Lord is Christ, head of the body, who fills all things (1:23) and is the source and goal of the church's growth (4:15-16). Earlier in Ephesians (2:8-9) we saw that faith referred to the human response of trust and obedience to God's initiative in Christ. Because of the connection with baptism here, most commentators see 4:5 referring to the public confession of faith that was a part of the baptismal experience (that is to say, a person confessing "Jesus is Lord" and thus giving voice to the commitment of faith and trust). One baptism is affirmed not because Paul had a particular mode of baptism in mind, but because baptism was the ritual of initiation by which a person was incorporated into the body of Christ.

All these unities climax in 4:6 with the assertion of the oneness of God who is not only transcendent ("above all") but also immanent ("through all and in all"). When I read Paul's affirmations of God in these terms, they remind me of my experiences of worship when I lived in England. The Baptist church my wife and I attended was small, and in the intimacies of that chapel and the fellowship of the community I experienced a sense of God's immanence; God was present with us and for us. Because that Baptist church did not have an evening service, we would frequently attend Evensong at the cathedral in Oxford where I had a completely different sense of God's presence. With the high stone-vaulted ceilings and the beautiful music of the organ and boy's choir drawing my eyes and heart heavenward, I experienced a sense of the transcendence and wholly otherness of God, the creator and sustainer of the world.

In Paul's acclamation of monotheism, he acknowledges both aspects of God's nature. If we only experience and emphasize one side of God in our worship and theologizing, our understanding of God is limited. Because Paul sees God's oneness as the source and ground of the unity of the church, when the church is fragmented and divided, it makes belief in the one God less credible.

What shape does the oneness of the church take? It would be a mistake to confuse unity with uniformity and conformity. The constructive side of a close-knit community is that it provides a high level of support to its members. The circle that includes, embraces, nurtures, and protects, however, can also exclude people. The constrictive side of community is experienced when it tries to enforce conformity and uniformity. Those who do not "fit" end up marginalized, even excluded, from the community. Paul certainly did not view the unity of the church as a bland oneness of uniformity and conformity, however, for immediately following the affirmations of the unities that constitute the oneness of the church, he sounds the note of diversity (4:7-16). The unity of the church includes a diversity that not only brings richness to community life, it makes it possible for the church to grow and mature. Diversity is as essential to the church's well-being as unity.

As Paul begins to discuss the diversity within the unity, he stresses the contributions and responsibilities of every member of the church. Grace was given to each individual in varying measure or proportion (4:7). Commentators agree that "grace" is used here not to mean God's saving initiative as we find elsewhere in Ephesians (see 2:8 for example). Rather, it parallels how the word *charisma,* "gifts," is used in Romans 12:3-12 and 1 Corinthians 12:4-11 where Paul lists the diversity of spiritual gifts in the church. The word grace does highlight, however, that these gifts have God as their ultimate source. This recognition should contribute to qualities, such as humility listed earlier (4:1-3), that help maintain and sustain the unity of the church.

To support his idea about Christ's gift, Paul quotes Psalms 68:18 in 4:8 in a curious way. The quotation in Ephesians is different from the text in the Old Testament.

In the Septuagint, which is the Greek translation of the Old Testament, the psalmist talks about a victorious king who "received" gifts from foes vanquished in battle. In Ephesians, gifts are given. Some Jewish interpretations of this psalm change the word to "gave" and apply it to Moses who ascended to heaven and gave the Torah as gifts to humans.

The idea of ascent in this verse suggests to Paul a corresponding descent (4:9-10). But to what does this descent refer? Three possible interpretations have been offered. Some see it as Christ's descent into Hades after his crucifixion (cf. 1 Pet 3:18-21; Rom 10:6-7). Others argue that the reference is to the descent of the incarnation in which God has become human in Jesus (see John 3:13; 6:62). The theme of humiliation-exaltation found in the hymn to Christ in Philippians 2:6-11 might represent a different use of the same ideas. The third option, and the one I find most convincing, is to understand the descent as the gift of the Holy Spirit. Although it is unusual to refer to the gift of the Spirit at Pentecost as the giving of Christ, Christ and Spirit are used interchangeably by Paul (see Rom 8:9-11), and it is through the Spirit that the risen Christ is present and active in the church. This line of interpretation also has the advantage of fitting the context with its emphasis of spiritual gifts.

Whichever line of interpretation we follow, however, the main emphasis of the quotation is not the descent but the ascent of Christ. The risen Christ whose rule is of cosmic significance gives the gift of the Spirit and the spiritual gifts to the church (4:10). Ephesians 4:11-16 explores both the nature of the gifts and the goal of the gifts. In this section we find side by side an emphasis on particular gifts with a recognition that every member has an indispensable role in the church. Church membership for Paul does not mean that one has his or her name somewhere on a church roll, but that every member contributes to the mission and growth of the church.

In the gifts we do find an emphasis on what might be called the teaching ministry of the church (4:11). Apostles and prophets, who have been mentioned earlier, serve as the foundation of the church (see 2:20). Evangelists would preach the gospel (the Greek word *euangelion*) and be involved in what we think of as mission work starting churches. Although in the Greek the words "pastors" and "teachers" share a definite article, I do not think they are identical. It is better to see the two having overlapping functions of leadership with local congregations in helping them grow to maturity.

Why this emphasis on what I have termed the teaching ministry? It is this ministry that transmits the apostolic traditions on which the church is built and then interprets and applies this tradition in the context of a local congregation. These people are particularly important because they help maintain unity. Moreover, if the church is to grow up to maturity in Christ, they must function as "enablers" who equip all Christians (the meaning of "saints" in 4:12) to carry out the work of ministry and so build up the body of Christ. To be a church member is not a spectator sport because all participate in the church's ministry. Ephesians provides us with a helpful perspective in understanding the role of clergy and laity in churches today. There is a need not only to preserve the "apostolic" tradition, but also to adapt it and creatively apply it in new situations so that all members of the church may be effective ministers.

Does the list in 4:11 represent offices in the church so that the people with these names have a specific position in the community, or are they functions that certain people may periodically (or even regularly) perform in the church? Margaret MacDonald argues in her book *The Pauline Churches* that Ephesians occupies a middle position between some of Paul's letters (for example, Romans, 1 and 2 Corinthians, Galatians, and so on) and the Pastorals (1 and 2 Timothy, Titus). With regards to the ministry, the undisputed Pauline letters reflect community-building institutionalization in which various ministries are given by God for people to perform and thus build the church. The Pastorals, on the other hand, reflect a community-protecting institutionalization. The church now exists as an institution with offices that have "job descriptions" and are considered necessary for the ongoing life of the church. The perspective of Ephesians falls between these two approaches and represents community-stabilizing institutionalization.

We find no evidence of ordination to office such as that in the Pastorals, and yet the people who are called evangelists, pastors, or teachers so regularly exercised these ministries that the church recognized them. In a period of community-stabilizing institutionalization, the church began to moderate its expectation of the imminent end of the world and develop a more long-term perspective. As we shall see, the use of the so-called household code in Ephesians 5:21-6:9 reflects this move with its concern of maintaining the church's distinctive identity within societal customs.

What is the goal of the various gifts given by Christ? Paul states it negatively in 4:14 that the church might not be immature like children. Childishness is characterized by a lack of direction and instability (the image of a storm-tossed boat at the mercy of wind and waves) and thus a susceptibility to error. The nature of the false teaching is not specified, but the warning of 5:6-13 ("let no one deceive you with empty words") suggests that Paul is worried about some of the ethical consequences of the teaching.

Positively, the goals of the gifts are unity, maturity, and growth to the stature of the fullness of Christ (4:13). Maturity is understood to be a corporate rather than an individual adulthood (notice, for example, the singular "person" used in conjunction with maturity in v. 13 in contrast to the plural "children" in v. 14). Paul is thinking about the church as a completed body here (cf. 2:15 where the church is "one new man") and not a collection of individuals. Similarly, the church is already the fullness of Christ (1:23), but it must become completely what it is already in principle. Although maturity and fullness are ascribed to the church, they cannot be separated from Christ. Christ is in the church (or even better perhaps, the church is in Christ). The church is the place where Christ is present and rules.

The process and goal of growth are summarized in 4:15-16. The standard of completeness toward which the church moves is not, according to A.. T. Lincoln, "just some potential inherent in its own existence but is Christ himself, the church's head."[2] Christ's headship means not only that he rules the church, but that he is also its origin and source. (We use language similarly when we describe the origin of a river as its "head.") The theme of unity in diversity is sounded again because, for growth to occur, every member of the church must contribute (that is to say, "each part is working properly"). Moreover, the church is active and not passive in this process of growth (it "upbuilds itself").

Finally, love is the indispensable means that makes unity (see 4:2) and growth possible (notice how the idea of "love" brackets 4:15-16). Paul combines in 4:15 "truth" and "love," not as competing qualities that hold each other in check, but as mutually sustaining qualities. "Speaking the truth in love" is more than just verbal accuracy; it also includes speech and actions that are genuine and authentic. For Paul, love "is the embodiment of the truth" and is "at the heart of the proclamation of the truth."[3] Too often in church we ask the question if something "is true" without asking the corresponding question "is it loving?" For the church to be vital and growing, Ephesians suggests that we not be unloving in our pursuit of truth, although neither should we be indifferent to truth in our attempt to be loving. Ultimately, however, the criterion of church unity and growth is not orthodoxy or numbers on church rolls, but a church characterized by love (cf. Eph 5:1-2).

Walking Distinctly
The Old and New Life
(4:17–5:20)

In Ephesians 4:17 Paul turns to provide specific examples of behavior that are appropriate to his readers' calling and new identity. In a sense, he returns to the concerns of 4:1-3 (notice the repetition of the idea of "walking" in 4:1 and 4:17). The intervening discussion between these verses about the nature and unity of the church should not simply be considered a digression by Paul, however. It underscores the idea that Paul's ethics are grounded in God's redemptive work in Christ and the Christian's incorporation into Christ. The ethic thus has a social or ecclesial dimension to it.

Paul's ethical advice is introduced by 4:17-24, which contrasts the old person with the new. Because he uses the imagery of undressing and dressing (see 4:22-24 and the language of "putting off" and "putting on"), many commentators see his advice drawing upon features of the early church's baptismal practices. When a person was baptized, the old dirty clothes would be stripped off to be replaced by a white gown as that person came from the waters. This new dress symbolized the newness of life for the Christian. Paul's ethical advice in this portion of Ephesians is in essence then exhorting his readers to live out the significance of their new identity. This advice also utilizes the same schema of then/now that we observed earlier in Ephesians. It almost represents an ethical version of chapter 2, for example. Distinctive Christian living is urged by contrasting their former way of life as Gentiles (that is to say, pagans) with a new way of life that is shaped by the pattern of Jesus (cf. Eph 5:6-14 where the contrast is between darkness and light).

The description of the old life (4:17-19) uses language similar to descriptions of pagan life found in Jewish apologetic works that extol the superior morality of Judaism. The former way of life is characterized by a distorted or darkened intellectual perception, a dullness of moral sensitivity, and a debased life. Paul's argument seems to be that just as the callouses that form on a manual worker's hand harden to deaden the pain of exertion, so the excesses of the old way of living dull the moral compass that gives ethical guidance.

The positive side of the contrast is found in Paul's urging for distinctive Christian living to be shaped after the pattern provided by Jesus and taught by the church (4:20-21). The new life involves a stripping off of the old life because its corrupting ways will eventually destroy. It also involves continual renewal of the mind. The Greek syntax of the sentence suggests that this action is a continual process. Too often people want to limit the Christian life to a one-time decision made at an altar without realizing that the decision must be renewed every day of a person's life. Although Ephesians 4:23 describes the renewal "from the inside out," Paul believes that this inward renewal will be evident in outward actions that are characterized by righteousness and holiness (4:24).

Paul's perspective on the new person in these verses is similar to what we saw earlier in his vision of the church. The new life is presented as both a reality and as a goal for his readers. It thus combines the polarities of gift and demand that constitute Christian existence. God's gracious initiative is present because the Christian is created by God, but humans are also responsible because they must put on the new person (4:24).

Paul follows the programmatic statement of 4:17-24 with a series of contrasting commandments. The distinctive holiness and ethical living of Christians are primarily illustrated in two areas: speech and sexual morality. With their new identity, Christians are to give up falsehood (4:25), hostility (4:26), evil talk (4:20), bitterness, wrath, anger, and malice (4:31). All are fundamentally antisocial in nature and destructive of community (as is stealing in 4:28).

The old adage "sticks and stones can break my bones, but words can never hurt me" is simply not true. Words can also wound, and speech that is deceptive and dishonest leaves scars. They can damage reputations, harm relationships, and ruin careers. Indulging anger by letting it fester under the surface of relationships Paul considers sinful because such anger has become an obsession that controls a person's life (4:26). This anger may eventually burst forth in the evil talk that Paul condemns. Because people know one another in the fellowship of a community such as church, the urge to gossip and share "news" about others may be tempting, but it is also characteristic of the old life and destructive to the new humanity created by God.

Paul contrasts such use of speech with the new life in which Christians speak the truth (4:25), do honest work so they can share with each other (4:28), speak so as to build up one another in their new identity (4:29), and be kind and loving to one another (4:32–5:2). The striking exhortation to "be imitators of God" (5:1) can be made because the readers are to put on a new identity that has been created in the "likeness of God" (4:24). The characteristics of the lives of Christians should share the qualities that characterize God. As a summary of these qualities of God, Paul exhorts his readers to live a life of forgiveness and sacrificial, self-giving love because this is the sort of love they have experienced from Christ (5:2). In contrast to the earlier lists of behavior and attitudes of the old life, the qualities of the new life build up the community of the church by creating trust and nurturing a sense of solidarity.

Sexual morality is the second area that Paul discusses to illustrate the distinctive holiness of Christian living (5:3-14), and some of his earlier concerns about speech and actions are carried forward here. The imagery of light and darkness is utilized to contrast the behavior of members in the community and those outside the community (5:6-14). Not only is sexual immorality condemned (5:3, 5), but coarse and obscene talk is also forbidden. Although such advice may seem prudish in the permissive climate of the present day, for Paul, this kind of talk is incompatible with the new identity Christians have in Christ. It is a part of the old dominion of darkness (5:8-10). His concern, in part at least, also seems to be that such talk can create an ethos in which sexual morality is more easily tolerated. Instead, the distinctiveness of the Christian's life is to be such that it proves to be a beacon of light that bears witness in the midst of darkness (5:11-13). Christians themselves have experienced such light in the newness of life they have in Christ, and his power continues to serve as light in their witness (5:14).

Paul's exhortation to thanksgiving in Christian speech (5:4) is the one positive note that contrasts with the surrounding lists of vices. While obscene talk, sexual immorality, and covetousness are selfish and self-centered, an attitude and speech characterized by thanksgiving are not (cf. 5:19-20). Instead of viewing objects and other people as things that exist for a person's pleasure and self-gratification (which is the attitude at the center of sexual immorality, for example), thanksgiving has God at the center of one's existence. It acknowledges God as the creator and sustainer of all and leads to the type of speech and actions that are loving because thanksgiving recognizes others as God's fellow creatures.

The experience of the Spirit is crucial to such a lifestyle (5:18). The joyous and thankful life comes not from being filled with wine (whose excesses lead to drunkenness and a loss of self-control), but to the filling of the Spirit. The characterization of this type of living as "wise" (Eph 5:15-17) draws upon the image of wisdom in the Old Testament. According to Martin, it "is not so much an intellectual achievement as an attitude toward life" that begins with God and allows a person to understand and appreciate life's pleasures as well as its pains.[4]

The filling of the Spirit also manifests itself in the joyous corporate worship. Ephesians 5:19-20 is one of those passages that provides us with a snapshot of worship in the early church. Music and songs move people not simply in a sentimental fashion (remember our earlier discussion that in biblical anthropology the "heart" was the center of a person's will and not the organ of emotion), but in praise and gratitutde. They thus help construct a vision of the alternative world in which God has so graciously acted and rules. The grace and gift of Christian ethics that undergird the demands of this section of the letter are reinforced in the experience of worship. The distinctive holiness of Christian living in this world springs from their identity God has provided.

Conclusion

How does the vision of the church in Ephesians as one body with Christ as the head, of unity in diversity with every member actively participating and growing in love, relate to the fragmented and divided condition of both Christendom and individual churches? Many theologians respond by making a distinction between the invisible and the visible church. Andrew Lincoln argues that a

> better distinction is to talk of the essence of the Church, uniting the ideal and the real, and the historical expression of this essence which is always partial, incomplete and broken.[5]

The church is fragmented and incomplete because it exists in the world on this side of the culmination of history. The vision of the church in Ephesians serves to call the church to strive to be a more complete expression of this essence God has created. Paul was no doubt aware of problems and conflicts within the church when he wrote Ephesians so that the church, as well as individuals, lives between the times in the tension between the "already" and the "not yet."

For those interested in ecumenical discussions, Ephesians may offer some guidelines. Paul's emphasis on diversity within unity suggests that ecumenicity should not be equated with uniformity. Moreover, if we extend by analogy to the church what Paul says about the diversity of spiritual gifts, we should allow the gifts of different Christian traditions to enrich the unity of the whole (cf. Eph 4:6). Finally, different traditions will need to be persistent in practicing the very qualities Paul urges in the interest of unity—especially love (see Eph 4:2-3, 15; 5:2).

Because this section of the letter is filled with practical concerns on how Christians should live out their new identity, the emphasis falls more squarely on the demand than on the gift side of Christian existence. The demands are only part of the picture, however. The demands for distinctive Christian living are not only a goal that Christians appropriate by their actions; they are also the gift of God. As "children of light," Christians stand out from the darkness of the world, but they do so by reflecting the light of God's grace in Christ (see Eph 5:11-14). Their distinctiveness is thus determined by God and not by the darkness and values of the world. Paul is not interested in a Christian withdrawing from the world as we shall see in his discussion of the household code (5:21–6:9) and spiritual warfare (6:10-20).

Questions for Reflection

1. What is the relationship between the first half of Ephesians and its theme of identity with the second half of Ephesians and its focus on ethics?
2. What is the difference between unity and uniformity in the church? Where is the unity of the church found?
3. What function or value does diversity have in the life of the church? Where is diversity found? What kind of different gifts do you see in your church?
4. What is the supreme event for Paul that defines God's love? How can you "imitate God" in your actions?

Notes

[1] Robert Coles, *The Spiritual Life of Children* (Boston: Houghton Mifflin, 1990) 19-20.

[2] Andrew T. Lincoln, *Ephesians*, Word Biblical Commentary, 42 (Waco TX: Word, 1990) 266.

[3] Ibid., 260.

[4] Ralph P. Martin, "Ephesians," *Broadman Bible Commentary* (Nashville TN: Broadman, 1971) 65.

[5] A. T. Lincoln and A. J. M. Wedderburn, *The Theology of the Later Pauline Letters* (Cambridge: Cambridge University Press, 1993) 154.

Chapter 5

Duties of the New Life

Ephesians 5:21–6:20

Like Paul, this writer still argues from elements at the center of his gospel, here particularly the lordship of Christ, and applies them in a way that neither immediately demolishes nor baptizes as Christian the social structures of his time but rather transforms them from within. The Ephesians household code, and particularly this part of it, serves as a reminder that Christians will always need to bring to bear the lordship of Christ on their everyday life in its social and economic concreteness, even though specific expressions of this will become obsolete as social conditions change and new forms of obedience need to be found.

—*Andrew T. Lincoln*

This study guide on Ephesians is being written during an election year. We have been bombarded with the theme of "family values" by all candidates in both political parties. Why do we find rhetoric on this theme? According to the speeches, the very stability and strength of America as a nation is at stake with the variety of issues relating to family and home that fall under this broad umbrella.

As Paul continues his exhortations about the character of the new life of Christians in Ephesians 5:21, we find him addressing what might be called "family values." He utilizes a form that scholars call "the household code." This form of exhortation was common in the ancient world and was utilized to address sets of relationships and responsibilities within society. By using this form to give ethical advice to his readers, Paul clearly implies that the new life of Christians does not involve nor necessitate their withdrawal from society.

We may need to remind ourselves at this point, however, that Paul did not write Ephesians in a vacuum. It is a letter that reflects its first-century setting, and society in the twentieth century is different from society in the first century. As we explore what the household code in Ephesians may mean to twentieth-century readers, therefore, it will be helpful to keep in mind what these "family values" meant to a first-century reader.

Duties in the Household
(5:21–6:9)

One of the basic units of Greco-Roman society in the first century was the household. It consisted not only of the immediate family, but was extended to include as well slaves and freedmen, even tenants and business associates at times. The household was a hierarchical and patriarchal body under the authority and rule of the father. Proper household management was viewed as crucial not only for the stability of the household, but also for the stability of society. Any upsetting of the hierarchy posed a threat to the state. Ethicists since the time of Aristotle therefore frequently gave advice to males about how to govern their wives, children, and slaves. This advice about proper household management also had a religious dimension. Members of the household were expected to follow the religion of the household's head (see, for example, the description of Cornelius and his household in Acts 10:2 or the conversion of the Philippian jailer and his household in Acts 16:29-34 where the household followed the religion of its head). Thus, any religion that attracted converts who were female or slave was seen as politically subversive. Clearly, obedience to the male head of the household was the norm. Women nowhere enjoyed the status, social freedoms, and autonomy that are widely recognized in America today. The first-century Jewish historian Josephus could write, for example, that according to the Law, the woman "is in all things inferior to the man. Let her accordingly be obedient, not for her humiliation, but that she may be directed; for God has given authority to the man."[1] Marriages were frequently arranged, and the wife was usually considerably younger than her husband. One of the greatest virtues a wife could possess was quiet submission to her husband (see Sirach 26:14, which describes "a silent wife" as "a gift from the Lord").

For children, parents—especially fathers—possessed status and exercised the authority of a superior over an inferior. According to the Hellenistic Jewish philosopher Philo,

> Parents . . . are to their children what God is to the world, since just as He achieved existence for the nonexistent, so they in imitation of His power, as far as they are capable, immortalize the race.[2]

The father had responsibilities for his children's education, and in the Roman legal system the father functioned as a magistrate in the family with power to impose various penalties. Dionysius of Halicarnassus, for example, praised the Roman notion of family life and education when he wrote,

> The lawgiver of the Romans gave virtually full power to the father over his son, whether he thought proper to

imprison him, to scourge, him, to put him in chains, and keep him at work in the fields, or to put him to death.[3]

Although these draconian measures were not always exercised, the expectation for children, in short, was that they obey their fathers.

Slaves, the third group addressed in the household code, were considered part of the householder's possessions. Aristotle, for example, argued there can be no talk of friendship or justice between master and slave because "there is nothing common to the two parties; the slave is a living tool and the tool a lifeless slave."[4] Despite this perspective, slaves were not necessarily treated as badly as our twentieth-century perceptions of slavery might assume. Slavery was widespread, and slaves performed a variety of jobs from manual labor to skilled positions. In addition, they had a number of different statuses and rights. It was possible for them to own property, marry, or even act as one's own legal person once they had been manumitted or set free by their owner. The apparent lack of interest here in Ephesians, as we also find elsewhere in the New Testament, in working to abolish slavery must be seen against the backdrop of first-century attitudes toward slavery.

Paul's ethical advice in Ephesians 5:21–6:9 where he uses the household code thus needs to be set in this first-century context. The three categories of relationships addressed in the list—wife/husband, child/father, and slave/master—reflect prevailing cultural assumptions and practices. It assumes a male-centered perspective (the analogy between Christ and the church, for example, makes Christ the model for the husband and the church the model for the wife). In every case, the subordinate member of the relationship is addressed first.

Despite what Paul had said earlier in Ephesians about the contrast in behavior between Christians and unbelievers (see 4:17-19 or 5:6-14, for example), Christian behavior in these areas, at least outwardly, appears very conventional and patriarchal. Christians are not to withdraw from the world but to live respectable and orderly lives in the everyday structures of society. Why? Did Paul believe like some contemporary Greek or Jewish ethicists that the household formed a basic building block of society and was thus crucial to its stability? Or was he concerned that the church not cause offense to others by its actions and thus be charged as a subversive institution? By having wives, children, and slaves submit, the church might avoid social ostracism and silence cultural objections to the gospel.

Paul, however, also brings Christian motivations of love and servanthood to the ethic that make his perspective stand out against the usual conventionalities of the ancient household code. First, Paul begins the household code in an unusual way in Ephesians 5:21. Syntactically, this transitional verse with its exhortation to "submit to one another" utilizes a participle that is dependent upon the verb "be filled" in 5:18. The exhortations about relationships in the household that follow are generally part of the new life that can be characterized as "wise" (5:5), but more specifically they are a continuation of the series of injunctions about spirit-filled living.

The appeal for mutual submission makes the transition from Paul's exhortations to the community in general (5:18-20) to his advice to specific groups in the community. The idea of mutual submission, however, stretches the normal sense of submission found in household codes. The introduction of the analogy of Christ and the church to support both his appeals for wives to submit to their husbands and husbands to love their wives gives the code a different character and motivation for actions than what we commonly find in Greco-Roman household codes (cf. Col 3:18–4:1, which does not have the opening exhortation for mutual submission).

Second, we find a striking degree of reciprocity in the Ephesians household code. Most Greco-Roman household codes were directed to the male head of the household with instructions about governing. In Ephesians, wives, children, and slaves are addressed first. Moreover, they are addressed as moral agents with a degree of autonomy who can voluntarily submit to the authority figure of the household.

Finally, after explaining the how and why slaves should submit to masters (6:5-8), Paul exhorts masters to "do the same" to slaves (6:9). The appeal to mutual submission in 5:21 is reinforced by an appeal to the principle of divine impartiality that does not make judgments based on social distinctions (6:9). The result is that the relationships and conventions of the household code are once both accepted and modified. Gerd Theissen has labeled this ethos in the church as "love patriarchalism" because social differences are allowed to stand, but the relationships are transformed by the new identity Christians have in Christ.

The appeal for mutual submission in Ephesians 5:21 that introduces the household code also contains the special Christological ground and motivation for Paul's exhortation. Christians are to submit to one another out of "fear of Christ." The idea of fear does not mean Christians are to be afraid or horrified of Christ, but the word also carries a stronger connotation than just "respect." Barth argues in his commentary that submission has a sense of obligation that springs forth from reverence or awe.

Paul gives the relationship between husbands and wives the most extensive treatment of the three relationships discussed in the household code (5:22-33). Wives are addressed first with a twofold appeal for them to submit to their husbands (vv. 22, 24). The basis of their submission, however, is not simply that these are the social structures of society. Rather, by submitting to the husband Paul asserts that the wife is also serving her Lord. The analogy of Christ and the church is introduced between the two appeals (5:23) and becomes the basis for the repetition of the appeal to submit in 5:24. Headship in these verses should primarily be understood in terms of authority, so that willing obedience by both the wife and the church is seen as an aspect of submission. Even if the appeal to submit is not based upon conventional social mores in the first century, Paul's use of the analogy of Christ and the church has the effect of reinforcing those mores as the wife's role is compared to the role of the church.

Most of the advice in this section of the household code, however, is directed to the husband. It also has a double appeal (5:25-27 and 5:28-32). The exhortation is not for the husband to rule his wife, which one might have expected after the earlier appeal for wives to submit, but to love (5:25). The warrant of the appeal is Christ's self-giving love for the church. Earlier in Ephesians this type of love was demanded for all believers (see 1:4; 3:17; 4:2, 15-16; 5:2), but now it is specifically demanded of husbands in relation to their wives. Ephesians 5:25-27 sets out the nature of Christ's love for the church that was given in order to make the church holy. The imagery of cleansing and purity may have baptismal overtones, but its bridal imagery may also draw upon the imagery of Ezekiel 16:8-14, which depicts God's relationship to Jerusalem in terms of a bride being presented to the bridegroom. The idea of sanctification in these verses, however, is not applied to individuals but to the church as a community.

Although in these verses Paul builds upon what he has said earlier in Ephesians about the nature of Christ and his church (see, for example, 1:22; 4:15 where Christ is the head of the church; or 3:19 and 5:2 where he gives himself in love for the church by his saving death [1:7; 2:14-18]), the purpose of the passage is to exhort believers to specific conduct. Paul's depiction of Christ's love for his church in 5:25-27 thus serves as the model for the husband's love for his wife in 5:28. The second appeal to love is extended first by the assertion that in such an action the husband also loves his own body. Paul's thinking at this point may be governed by his quotation later of Genesis 2:24 that husband and wife become one flesh, or he could be returning to the analogy of Christ and the church since the church has been identified earlier in Ephesians as Christ's body.

The appeal to love is further extended by the assertion that the husband who loves his wife nourishes and cherishes his own body (5:29-30). This assertion seems to leave no room for an asceticism that denigrated marriage. Many commentators think this type of attitude that denied the role of sexual relations between husbands and wives may have been behind the advice about marriage found in Ephesians (cf. Col 2:16-23 and 1 Cor 7:1-7 for examples of ascetic behavior in the early church).

The quotation of Genesis 2:24 in 5:31-32 brings together the various threads of Paul's argument since verse 28. Paul's advice about marriage is based upon the idea of husband and wife becoming one flesh. More important, however, his use of Christ and the church provides him an appropriate model because he sees Genesis 2:24 "as referring to the profound mystery that God has now revealed in Christ, namely, the union between Christ and the church."[5] The union between husband and wife thus reflects in its own way the unity of the church that is a part of God's purposes for the world (cf. Eph 1:9 and 3:9 where mystery is also used).

In conclusion, Paul's advice in Ephesians 5:22-33 provides us with an exalted view of marriage. This passage gives no sense of marriage as an option that is second best, as in the impression created by 1 Corinthians 7 where Paul's preference is clearly for celibacy. Although the external roles and duties of marriage may look very similar to the conventional roles of marriage in first-century Greco-Roman society, the Christological grounding and motivation of marriage based upon the relationship between Christ and his church should give Christian marriage a dynamic that is quite different from the prevailing ethos. Just as there is diversity within the unity of the church, self-giving love and voluntary submission both expressed in a relationship of mutual submission give Christian marriage its unity.

The next pair of relationships addressed in the household code is that between children and parents (6:1-4). Children are addressed first and enjoined to obey their parents. The warrants for this obedience are natural law ("this is right"; 6:1) and the fifth of the Ten Commandments (6:2-3). The male-centered perspective of the code is evident when parental responsibilities are addressed only to the father (6:4). Negatively, fathers are not to abuse their authority by provoking their children to anger. Positively, they are exhorted to train and discipline their children. The Christological motivation for this upbringing is found in the expression "of the Lord." What is remarkable about this section of the household code vis-à-vis prevailing cultural norms is the restraint of harsh parental authority. No mention is made of corporal punishment, for example, which would be common in much contemporaneous Greco-Roman or Jewish advice about parenting (cf. the number of sayings in Prov 13:24; 23:13-14, for example, which warn against sparing "the rod" with children).

The last pair of relationships found in the household code is between slaves and masters (6:5-9). As with the other pairs, the subordinate party is addressed first. Unusual is the way slaves are addressed as full, responsible members of the Christian community. The advice to them is general—obey your earthly masters (6:5)—but the motivation throughout is profoundly Christian and Christological. They are addressed as "slaves of Christ" (6:6} who are to serve earthly masters "as to Christ" (6:5) or "as to the Lord" (6:7). Masters are exhorted to do likewise (6:9) with the result that the focus on Christ throughout the passage relativizes the social distinctions usually found in household codes.

Because this last set of exhortations to slaves and masters more clearly reflects its first-century setting than the other appeals about marriage and children, it raises the question more vividly perhaps of how twentieth-century Christians should appropriate Paul's advice when we live in a society where slavery is no longer practiced. Andrew Lincoln argues that the church should avoid the two extremes of either ignoring the advice because it is no longer relevant or too easily modernizing it by making it say something about the relationship of employers to employees. At the bare minimum, the passage reminds us that all Christians are full and equal members of the church no matter what their social status may be.

With regard to parents and children, the passage can warn us to avoid the extremes of either abuse of parental power or avoiding the exercise of parental authority. The ideal is a relationship of mutual respect that is appropriate to both parent and child.

How can twentieth-century readers appropriate the view of marriage in Ephesians 5? Is Paul providing us with a universal prescription for marriage? To answer these questions, it is important first of all to realize that the picture of marriage in Ephesians 5:22-33 is an ideal in which both husband and wife accept the lordship of Christ as well as their respective roles. It has nothing to say, for example, about what to do when the husband refuses to love his wife in the self-giving way that Christ loved the church. We also need to recognize that the perspective of the code is male-centered. Why do we need to assign love only to one partner and submission to another? Surely wives can also love their husbands with the self-giving love of Christ.

Andrew Lincoln argues that the more responsible way for modern readers of Ephesians to appropriate its advice is to do what Paul did in the letter and "bring to bear on the marriage conventions of the day what is held to be the heart of the Christian message."[6] Even in a male-dominant culture, the household code challenged traditional male dominance (see 5:21). At the heart of the gospel is found a radical egalitariaism (see Gal 3:28). Mutual loving submission thus becomes the way in which the unity of marriage is demonstrated. Love and submission should be seen as "two sides of the same coin—selfless service of one's marriage partner."[7] In this way marriage is prevented from becoming a relationship of competing rights between partners. The ideal of permanent "one flesh" union also serves to provide the firm foundation of trust and commitment that is so necessary for personal growth and love to flourish. The analogy between Christ and the church challenges "the notion that relationships exist for personal profit and can be discarded when they fail to yield enough."[8]

Standing Firm in Spiritual Warfare
(6:10-20)

Paul concludes his instruction about how Christians are to live out their new identity in Christ not with specific injunctions, but with general exhortations for Christians to stand firm and thus play their part in a wider cosmic battle. A letter that began with an emphasis on the present experience of salvation thus ends with imagery of warfare. Despite the emphasis in Ephesians on the realized nature of salvation, its conclusion warns against assigning a naive optimism to its author. The world in which Christians live is not viewed as neutral ground but a battlefield.

The passage divides neatly into three sections: (1) 6:10-13 exhorts the readers to be strong and stand firm in the battle by reminding them that God's armor provides them with strength, (2) 6:14-17 provides more detail about the pieces of God's armor, and (3) 6:18-20 urges constant prayer as the means of standing firm and appropriating God's armor. The call to be strong in the opening section makes plain that the ultimate antagonists in the battle are God and the devil (see 6:11, 13 where it is the armor of God that enables believers to withstand attacks from the devil). God has provided Christians with all that is needed to withstand the attack. Every piece of armor listed in verses 14-17 serves a necessary function.

The idea of putting on the armor brings to mind the injunction for Christians to put off the old humanity and clothe themselves in the new humanity God has created (4:22-24). The tension between the "already" and "not yet" that is a part of the structure of Christian existence for Paul is thus also operative in this opening section. Previously, the readers would have been under the dominion of the principalities of this age, but because God has called them and given them a new identity in Christ, the battle has begun.

The picture of the armor of God that Christians are provided parallels the pieces of equipment that Roman soldiers used. The armor also reflects, however, pictures in the Old Testament of God as a mighty warrior. Isaiah 11:4-5; 49:2; 52:17; and 59:11, 16-17 all describe the armor or weapons of God or the Messiah. These Old Testament allusions may underscore for the readers that their protection not only comes from God, but is the very armor of God. Of the six pieces of armor described, the first four—truth, righteousness, peace, and faith—are all virtues that believers demonstrate. The final two—salvation and the Spirit—are gifts from God.

The first piece of equipment needed is the belt of truth. A belt was necessary for the soldier because it fastened clothing securely and made possible swift action in long, flowing garments. In Isaiah 11:5, righteousness and truth clothe the Messiah-King. Since the next three pieces of armor are all ethical virtues that believers demonstrate, the belt of truth here should probably be understood in a similar way as integrity and sincerity. Any collusion with untruths or half-truths by believers will entangle them and slow them down in the battle.

The second piece of armor is the breastplate of right-eousness. This piece is a part of God's armor in Isaiah 59:17. The breastplate protected a soldier's lungs and heart. The equivalent protection for Christians is found in upright and just conduct.

Proper footwear was necessary if a soldier was to be successful in battle. Roman soldiers wore half-boots with studs in the soles that helped give them firm footing. The third piece of equipment is described as having fitted your feet with the readiness of "the gospel of peace" (6:15). The language of this verse is difficult to understand and may have been influenced by Isaiah 52:7, which refers to "the feet of one preaching glad tidings of peace." What is the meaning of this image for Christians preparing for spiritual battle? According to C. Leslie Mitton, it means that Christians are "provided with tireless energy" because they have the good news of peace to bring to the world.[9] Andrew Lincoln, on the other hand, argues that the image refers to the firm footing Christians have as they prepare for battle. Since Christ "is our peace" (Eph 2:14-16), he provides a firm foundation against the fragmenting powers of evil.[10]

The fourth piece of armor is the shield of faith. The Greek word used for "shield" here refers to the large shield approximately four feet tall and more than two feet wide that a soldier would stand behind for protection for his entire body. Faith in this context does not refer to intellectual assent to particular doctrines, but to a person's act of commitment and trust in God. We should think of the word functioning as a verb rather than as a noun. For Christians, such commitment and trust in God and God's resources provide protection against every type of assault hurled at them by the "evil one."

The final two pieces of armor in the list refer to gifts from God rather than to virtues Christians demonstrate (6:17). First, Christians are equipped with the helmet of salvation. The language is drawn from Isaiah 59:17 where it is God who puts on the helmet. Here God provides salvation for the Christian. Just as the helmet protected the head, a vital organ for the Roman soldier, so the ultimate protection for Christians from the onslaught of the devil is the fact that God has already defeated the powers through Christ's death and resurrection (see Eph 2:5, 8). The realized nature of the Christian's salvation that we find in Ephesians thus comes into play here in the description of God's armor.

The one offensive weapon in the description of the armor of God is found in the final piece of equipment, the sword of the Spirit. This sword is further identified as the word of God. The Spirit not only supplies the sword, it also gives the word its effectiveness. What is the word here? It is probably the gospel message, for as Christians proclaim the gospel, they help overcome the evil forces in the world. Or, as Andrew Lincoln phrases it, "As the Church continues to be the reconciled and reconciling community, the gospel conquers the alienating hostile powers and brings about God's saving purposes."[11]

The Greek syntax of the final section (6:18-20) with its use of participles makes clear that this section stands in close connection with the description of the armor that has preceded. Prayer is not the seventh piece of equipment, however, but the means by which believers are to appropriate God's armor and stand firm in the battle. This prayer is to be constant and guided by the Holy Spirit, who provides access to God (see Eph 2:18). It does not come naturally to human nature, but involves discipline and should

be undertaken with an attitude of alertness and persever-
ance. Finally, such prayer is not offered only on behalf of
the one praying, but also petitions God to strengthen and
help others (6:18-20). Prayer should be seen as a community activity in which we have the privilege of supporting
our fellow Christians and sharing in both their joys and
tribulations.

Conclusion

Throughout the final section of Ephesians the imperative
for Christians to stand firm in the spiritual battle is repeated with the verb "to stand" (6:11, 13, 14). This verb
complements and completes the thought of other verbs that
characterize the different sections of the letter. In the first
half of the letter Paul addressed the identity and status of
Christians as the new people God has created and called.
Through prayer and thanksgiving Paul creates a world in
which Christians experience the present realities of salvation. Nowhere is this perspective better expressed than
when Paul describes Christians as already "sitting" with
Christ in the heavenly places (see 2:6).

The second half of the letter focuses on ethics and
repeatedly uses the verb "to walk" (see 4:1, 17; 5:2, 8, 15).
Here Christians are urged to live out the new identity and
calling God has given them. The ethical imperative is
rooted in the indicative of divine initiative and grace. It is
not simply an individualist ethic, however, for the new life
is to be lived out in community with others.

In summation with the final exhortation "to stand" in
battle (6:11, 13, 14), Paul combines the ideas in the previous
verbs. For Christians to be strong and victorious in the

battle, they need to appropriate the resources God has provided along with their new identity and live out this identity in struggle with the hostile powers of this age. Ephesians may not have the pathos of human suffering and weakness in the theology of the cross that we find in other places in the New Testament, but for readers with an inadequate sense of their new identity as Christians, Ephesians' vision of the church's role in God's purposes boosts their confidence in God's transforming power. Because their identity and resources for spiritual battle are provided by a God whose power is immeasurable (see 3:20), God is, according to Lincoln, "well able to take up the church's very imperfect and fragmented responses to his calling in achieving his purposes of unity and love for all."[12]

Questions for Reflection

1. Describe the social mores and structures of the first century that are addressed by the household code. How does Paul reinforce these structures as well as modify them?
2. Describe contemporary social mores and structures that are addressed by the household code. How would you bring the message of the gospel to bear upon these structures and mores today?
3. Paul describes the Christian in spiritual warfare against principalities and powers in 6:10-13. Who or what do you understand to be the evil spiritual powers that Christians battle against today?
4. List each piece of God's armor mentioned in 6:14-17 and its relevance for the spiritual battle. How are these resources utilized in your Christian walk?
5. Summarize the message of Ephesians for today's church.

Notes

[1]Cited by Andrew T. Lincoln, *Ephesians*, Word Biblical Commentary, 42 (Waco TX: Word, 1990) 357.

[2]Ibid., 399.

[3]Ibid., 398.

[4]Ibid., 416.

[5]Ibid.

[6]Andrew T. Lincoln, *Theology of the Later Pauline Letters*, 162.

[7]Lincoln, *Ephesians*, 393.

[8]Ibid.

[9]C. L. Mitton, *Ephesians*, New Century Bible (Grand Rapids MI: Eerdmans, 1973) 225-26.

[10]Lincoln, *Ephesians*, 449.

[11]Ibid., 451.

[12]Lincoln, *Theology of the Later Pauline Letters*, 166.